AMERICA'S MUSIC MAKERS

BIG BANDS & BALLROOMS 1912-2011

By John "Jack" Behrens

Author of the popular book,
Big Bands & Great Ballrooms
America is Dancing... Again
(AuthorHouse/2006)

AuthorHouse/2010

AuthorHouse™
1663 Liberty Drive
Bloomington, IN 47403
www.authorhouse.com
Phone: 1-800-839-8640

First published by AuthorHouse 3/2/2011

ISBN: 978-1-4567-2952-3 (sc)
ISBN: 978-1-4567-2951-6 (e)

Library of Congress Control Number: 2011901315

Printed in the United States of America

Any people depicted in stock imagery provided by Thinkstock are models, and such images are being used for illustrative purposes only. Certain stock imagery © Thinkstock.

This book is printed on acid-free paper.

For information visit: www.writerjackweb.com

Graphics and production were prepared by Lisi Design, Holland Patent, NY

Table of Contents

Prologue 5

Territorial Dance Bands: America's Unsung Music Makers 17

Ballrooms Made the Big Band Era 39

Big Band Road Warriors 59

Society Orchestras: Sweet Sounds Were Very Successful 79

Many Think the Beat Made Big Bands Popular 101

Theme Songs of the Big Bands 117

Reminisces of the Big Band Days 127

Acknowledgements 145

About the Author 149

Index 151

Cover photos: Jitterbug dancers, Chief Wah We-Otten and His Sioux Indian Orchestra, Louie Armstrong at Buckeye Lake, OH, Red Sievers' Orchestra, teenagers Jim Booker and the author practicing outside in the driveway when the house was off limits.

Back cover photo: Author Jack Behrens on drums (photo by Larry Pacilio)
Arrangements made by Kathy Randall and Utica College Media Center

Prologue

For those who have enjoyed contemporary music, whether dance band, jazz, swing, bop, or rock, it has been the constant in a world with little order, too much violence, death and too little rhythm. I discovered it at a manmade lake in Ohio and in a monthly magazine appropriately called *Downbeat*. I thought everybody who was anybody read it. It was my bible for years and it was gold to musicians whether you played occasionally or weekly.

It was so invaluable, in fact, that during my playing years when I couldn't afford the newsstand price I read it in the library. Sometimes, friends and I passed a dog-eared copy around from one to another. I was holding down two low paying jobs as a dairy bar clerk (sounds so much better than the insulting "soda jerk" label) and summer recreation aide to support my Friday night $20 "regular" gig playing for three hours in a well-rehearsed society band. To my father's consternation, that was my "steady" employment. Social Security had just begun taking an amount from our checks but for three summers at least I could count on Friday night dances at a place called the Sherman Armory in downtown Lancaster, OH. I played other gigs especially the holidays which gave me an incredible $1,000 gross income one year. But the government didn't appear to like such wealth in a musician's hands so the Social Security take continued to increase. It wasn't the income I told myself… it was playing time and the possibility of connecting with a "real" band that played the music I really dug! I remember a Toledo engagement I had where Barney Rapp, an Ohio bandleader/entrepreneur who discovered Rosemary Clooney among others, was in the crowd and our leader told us he was looking for a drummer and a trumpet player. Barney at least talked to me. At the break he told me and I remember his words to this day: "you're playing a bop beat and nobody wants a bop drummer." End of conversation… end of life for me!

But I wasn't completely lost because I still had steady gigs with a good society band and occasional one nighters with northern Ohio bands when I went back to college. Everybody's path to entertain was different, however. A pen pal of mine later in life was Lou DiSario aka Lou King. During civilian life he was a dance instructor, master of ceremonies/ singer and manager of the Million Dollar Pier at Atlantic City. Like millions of other American men he was inducted into military service in 1942 and he landed in the Pacific at New Caledonia where he lifted troop morale putting on Red Cross shows. Packed with his combat gear was his red zoot suit for countless USO shows. When he left the military, he turned down an offer from actress Ann Rutherford to go to Hollywood and returned to his native Philadelphia where he did tours with singers Billy Eckstine, Andy Williams, Frankie Laine, Dean Martin and the Harmonicats and became friends with Frank Sinatra.

Yet, he never forgot the guys he served with either. He volunteered to do shows at veterans medical centers throughout the Midwest and east for the rest of his life. His spirit for the music and the times continues.

Big band musicians gather at the Lyndon Elks Club, near Louisville, KY every Wednesday night and host a number of players each week who sit in. It's like a lodge meeting, some laugh. Contemporary music—dance band music—is alive and well in middle America too. Back in 2005 a guest of honor was 90-year-old Bob Wrege, a saxophonist, who told a Louisville *Courier-Journal* reporter that he won't stop playing. "It takes the place of being in a bowling league or something," he smiles. Laughter, good music played by guys who have been blowing horns, caressing the keyboard or playing drums for decades is as American as mom's apple pie.

And it comes alive everywhere musicians gather for fun. Listen to Al Croft who emailed me from Sedona, AR about how a city of 15,000 celebrates. "We've got our own territorial band called *Sentimental Journey*. A few years ago, the touring Gene Krupa Band, led by drummer Michael Berkowitz, with the current edition of the Four Freshmen filled a nearby college auditorium. All were admittedly mostly gray haired. We have a Phoenix high school band, *The Young Sounds*, which is sponsored by the local musicians' union. It's already recorded a number of CDs. Phoenix Community College sponsors a powerhouse big band with two exceptional vocalists. There is a good big band playing in Prescott, AZ and Phoenix is home to the Glenn Miller Alumni Orchestra and Northern Arizona University has an excellent jazz studies program too."

The excitement of the big bands is still a draw to young musicians who realize the opportunities are far different today than in the golden era of music.

The excitement of the big bands is still a draw to young musicians who realize the opportunities are far different today than in the golden era of music.

"I think I surprised Tex Beneke when I first met him with my questions," says young bandleader Alan Glasscock of Dallas, TX. "He was most accustom to the usual questions about Glenn Miller, what was your favorite recordings, etc. I show up and ask things like what about the actual Miller arrangements, saxophone voicings and recording techniques on sound tracks of Miller's two films, *Sun Valley Serenade* and *Orchestra Wives*," Alan told me. "I saw him in 1998 at the Dallas Big Band Festival. When he came onstage, he was the only star who got a standing ovation. He was obviously not in good health but after all, he was in his 80s and doctors had forbid him from playing his sax four years earlier. He had been a heavy smoker and his lungs were failing. Yet he still sang *Chattanooga Choo Choo*, *Ida Sweet As Apple Cider* and *Don't Sit Under the Apple Tree* and his singing was recognizable despite his appearance." After the show, Alan told Tex he was still available to do charts for Miller band but his response was unexpected. "Alan, he said, I'm not going to be adding anymore tunes… I'm not going to be around much longer." Tex Beneke died almost two years later from respiratory arrest in a California nursing facility.

The evolution of dance bands was closely associated with the national trend and the growth of dance pavilions. The first big band, some music historians claim, played its first gig in 1912 at Chicago's Pekin Theater, not exactly a dance hall. Wilber Sweatman, who could play clarinet, violin and even tinkle the piano, organized the group after spending a number of years as music director of several Windy City theaters. A self-taught musician (who wasn't in those days?). Wilber was multi-talented; he played three instruments at once during his vaudeville days. He also knew talent too. He gave Edward Kennedy "Duke" Ellington his beginning as a piano player a decade later.[1] From the early 1900s to the 1960s, communities throughout the United States had ballrooms; some were in hotels, some were stand alone buildings owned by groups, families and communities and still others were converted restaurants, night clubs, Elks Lodges, American Legion halls, country clubs, VFW buildings, corporate structures, high school gymnasiums, college student unions and various other facilities that could be easily converted for dancers in an evening.

But there were opponents to the music and the dancing. An American psychiatrist, Abraham Arden Brill, complained that swing music was decadent, created evil sensations and the beat of the tom-tom was a dangerous narcotic similar to opium. He wrote a piece in the *American Journal of Psychiatry* called *The Evil of Swing Music*, which discussed the emotional problems that such music could conjure. Brill emigrated to the United States from

Austria at 15 without his family and little money. He worked to support himself through high school and he graduated from New York University. He later joined the New York State Mental Hospital staff. His complaint didn't dissuade many although it did trouble the professional classes. Critics like Brill and others caused the territory musician and his music to rarely be recorded or written about. Society accepted such music reluctantly like narcotics or booze neither proud of it or ready to acknowledge it. Recognition came decades later.

The music, of course, came before the ballrooms but both were linked in America for decades to provide teens, middle aged and elderly melodies and rhythms and give Arthur Murray a thriving business teaching dance. And it shaped its own form; the well known one-nighter which began on an appointed hour (usually 9 p.m.) and ended in the wee hours of the morning. Soon, there were thousands of enthusiastic big band followers—chooches, Willie Schwartz called them—who would skip school, drive hundreds of miles or more to see one of the elite and savor the music and the experience. Dick Yeakel offers a classic response: "I saw Tex Beneke in person about 45 times. Castle Garden, Rainbow Room & Frolics Ballroom in Allentown, PA. Sunnybrook Ballroom in Pottstown, PA, Steel Pier in Atlantic City, Frank Dailey's Meadowbrook, Hershey Park Ballroom and many, many other places from 1947 up to 1999 at the Stardust in Las Vegas. I have many autographed photos and pictures of him including a few with me. When I saw him at Hershey Park and other ballrooms in 1951 Eydie Gorme was his girl singer. I've got every record he made and every CD that has been released. To me, the Tex Beneke band was the greatest dance band of all time. I'll miss him always. He was a great tenor saxman and a wonderful person. He always had a minute to talk to fans… a priceless asset in this day and age," Dick told me in an email.

There were thousands of struggling musicians throughout the country who had been motivated by the big band craze of the '30s, '40s and '50s and wanted to participate. A good example was a talented "Boy Trumpet Wonder" named B.A. Rolfe. He spent his teenage years on the road as a circus clown with Sparks Circus. At 18, he became a solo trumpet player with the Majestic Theater Orchestra in Utica, NY. A short time later, he was chosen brass instrument chair with the Utica Conservatory of Music and then he began a life touring concert halls and elegant ballrooms with some of America's top musical organizations. An entrepreneur at heart, B.A. was excited by the rise of motion picture and

B.A. Rolfe
Photo courtesy of Wikipedia.org

he used his savings to begin Rolfe Photoplays in New York City. The venture failed. After making nearly 100 silent films but his money exhausted, he declared

Promotional Poster for Jimmy Dorsey
Photo courtesy of Jack Henke

bankruptcy and sold what assets were left to Columbia Pictures. He returned to music and joined one of America's sweet bands at the time, Vincent Lopez ("Lopez Speaking") and spent the next 20 months traveling and playing along side such future artists as Artie Shaw, Xavier Cugat, Jimmy and Tommy Dorsey, Glenn Miller and singers Betty and Marion Hutton. He returned to Utica on a one nighter to play the Hotel Utica. Two years later, Rolfe got the support of Paul "Pops" Whiteman and organized a band. It's possible he was financed by Whiteman who had

a total of 68 bands under his name at the time, 11 of them in New York.[2]

It was a typical story of those with talent who were recruited to join well publicized touring bands of 10 to 18 pieces or society bands of 7 to 12 musicians playing weekly gigs for dancing pleasure. We didn't realize in the late 1940s what insiders already knew; the big band craze was nearly gone and the ballrooms, clubs and touring orchestras had nearly vanished with them in the post-war years.

What brought the drastic change in the musical landscape?

Years earlier, Paul Whiteman told critics and reviewers his view of the collapse of the big bands and the loss of the ballrooms. In Leo Walker's fascinating book, *The Wonderful Era of the Great Dance Bands (DaCapo, 1964)* Whiteman put the blame on the bandleaders themselves. "... you're digging our own graves' when singers were featured and crowds gather around the stand to listen instead of dancing. The bandleaders stopped playing dance numbers," he said. Ironically, Paul Whiteman was the first to feature singers—Morton Downey and Mildred Bailey—in his band. His defense was that "I made them sing in dance tempo. I didn't want to do anything to stop the dancing."

Yet, years later when touring orchestras had all but vacated playing sites there was still a strong demand for local bands playing memorable music for milestone events and holidays. Gary Greenfelder, leader of Detroit's popular *One Beat Back* band, says his mail and email demonstrate the group's importance to the community over the years.

A donor at annual swing dance for a charity fundraiser told Gary: "What a blast. I can't wait for next year's event. You are doing it again I hope!" Certainly money keeps bands in business but pleasing audiences is equal if not more important. "For me all of this is very exciting and there are plenty of opportunities to have a lot of fun doing what we love to do! Detroit's economy is very challenged and we are happy to be as busy as we are and also at having the potential to continue creating new shows and variety to keep our fans interested," he told me.

To make sure his band remains fresh and current, Gary creates a good blend of talent and music when the *One Beat Back* performs. "I try to have a little something for everyone, especially from the big band arena, including everything from Glenn Miller to Maynard Ferguson to Auturo Sandoval. We started a collection of Tom Kubis charts and with the addition of our male vocalist we've added about 28 Sinatra arrangements as well as a few from Dean Martin. Our focus is to stay with the music that sounds best in the big band instrumentation," he adds.

Gary Greenfelder
Photo courtesy of Gary Greenfelder

A latecomer to the scene in the 1950s was a creative and sophisticated band with soft tones managed by two talented brothers, Les and Larry Elgart.

I remember it as a piano-less band with strong section sounds and subdued rhythm. They arrived with fresh orchestrations as ballrooms from coast to coast were being dismembered, torched or simply closed down.

But the band survived the national meltdown. Their sound was clever enough to attract college bookers, Greek houses and campus dancers. While many mainstream bandleaders were selling off their charts, seeking semi-retirement and occasional freelance gigs, Les and Larry of New London, CT were letting their talent speak for itself to a younger generation. Les, the elder, played trumpet and later led his own group when the brothers split. He died in 1977.

Larry, meanwhile, is approaching his 90th birthday at this writing but he has remained active from his home in Long Boat Key, FL. He has been in the business long enough to remember his failures with his successes. He worked with the great Tommy Dorsey band, traveled with trumpeter Charley Spivak where I saw him, was a member of Woody Herman's fabled 1st Herd and played later with Freddie Slack, Bobby Byrne and Red Norvo. While a number of touring bands were disbanding in 1946, the Elgarts decided the time was right to start their organization. They had an edge; besides knowing the business better than most, they knew the people who could make such an enterprise successful. Their arrangers? Some of the country's best; Nelson Riddle, Bill Finegan and Ralph Flanagan.

First they called their group the "Elgart Sound." That was followed by something that caught fire from the beginning "Sophisticated Swing." Even later, they scored again with what they entitled "Hooked on Swing." It came after legendary Glenn Miller's time but I'm sure as an arranger Glenn would have applauded. Everything was crafted with danceable clean melodies and tempos and the woodwind section using staccato to give it something different.

Elgart music without a doubt is "feel good" music. Larry told reporter Jessica Luck of the *LongBoat Observer Key Life (March 15, 2007)* that his interpretation of music to dance to is shaped by the alto sax he plays. "It's a concept of the instrumentation of my own playing reflected throughout the band. There's a definite clarity to it, as everything that was played was done so to be recorded."

Wife Lynne, his business manager, says the sound, like Glenn Miller's distinctive sound, was the key to their success. To get it in the recording studio, technology played a role. Trombones came out of one speaker, for example, and rhythm came from the other… which created the quality sound they wanted for the hi-fidelity at Decca in the 1950s. MCA was so enthusiastic about the sound it pressed 3,000 demo copies of *Sophisticated Swing* when it was released, the largest promotion of a big band at that time. Larry won the Grammy in 1959 for the best recording of a big band sound and he got the special title of "Ambassador of Swing."

Did he earn it?

"I've been on the road since I was 15 sending home money to support my parents and my brother Les. It's a terrible business and a very rough road."

That sounds like a yes.

Musicians and bands, of course, have led in contributing to community charities and fundraisers. They frequently are the attraction and donate their time and perform for free or at a substantial low rate because of the cause and their commitment. They aren't always included in the thank yous, unfortunately, but they should be. Entertainers, if you examine both major wars this country fought and the continuing conflicts that American military have been involved in were the morale builders in World War I and II and also raised substantial monies for the country's war efforts. They continue to do so today.

Downbeat kept us in tune in the early days about the whereabouts of our favorite sidemen and bands and offered us the inside on an ever changing musical landscape, its leaders, trends, union squabbles and the personal battles of the stars. I'm sure *The Law Journal* and *CPA Review* weren't read and reread with as much zeal. Nat Hentoff and Leonard Feather, two veteran *Downbeat* writers, were the eyes and ears on our special world. The magazine was and continues to be a powerful tool to ambitious musicians who seek a career in a field considered to be as dangerous as a high wire circus act without a net. The risks were always there whether you were a territorial musician or a touring bandsman.

Listen to the great Stan Kenton, who some believed revolutionized the dance band by challenging people to listen to a different kind of music in the post-World War II and cold war periods and demanded that audiences understand the music musicians wanted to play, not the music people wanted to dance to necessarily.

He explained his difficulty and his battle with bookers, ballroom owners and promoters in the May 19, 1950 issue of *Downbeat*: "I had to book and promote my concert tour because the established agents and promoters were too scared to do it. I'll keep right on doing it myself until the agents and promoters wake up or until — and this is more likely — new blood appears in the field which is alive to the potentialities of the business today," he wrote adding that "It will be only with the appearance of new blood that we'll get away from the current obsession of trying to play a safe thing… There is no such thing as a 'safe thing' in the music business."

> *There is no such thing as a 'safe thing' in the music business.*

He was talking most assumed about the Lawrence Welks, the Jan Garbers, the Guy Lombardos and Sammy Kayes and other sweet bands who routinely played what audiences came to hear and do when they went out for an evening: dance.

Stan had his followers, of course. He had his zealots and I was one. I had met him as a 14-year-old in a parking lot of the Pier Ballroom at the

Buckeye Lake, OH Amusement Park where I was an eager volunteer band boy helping tote instruments, music charts and stands to the dance hall steps away for an evening's performance. Stan spent 45 minutes or so with me and didn't shoo me off as some would. He re-energized my desire to become a big band player in between telling me where certain containers had to go and asking where the bathroom facilities were. I met Gene Krupa, Harry James, Shep Fields, Blue Barron, Claude Thornhill, Charlie Spivak, Vaughn Monroe, Eddy Howard, Louis Prima and others in the same parking lot over a three to four year period as I eagerly took in the excitement of where they had been and what they did for a living. Some bands were in from Moonlight Gardens,

Vaughn Monroe
Photo courtesy of Buckeye Lake (OH) Museum

Cincinnati, the Palmer House or the Aragon, Chicago or others were overnight and headed west. They had come from Central New York where they played at Russells' Danceland on Oneida Lake, the Blue Note in New York City or the fabled Glen Island Casino just outside the city.

It was rare that I found an ill-tempered leader although some of the sidemen weren't exactly the most friendly. I remember a few who, when the bus driver unloaded their equipment on the pavement, weren't interested in a "kid" handling their instruments or even their suitcase. I remembered how tired they were and later in life when I was playing I could well understand the drain the trips, the one-nighters and the lack of food and sleep were although I rarely had a night where I didn't go home and sleep in my own bed.

Kenton played "progressive" music, critics wrote, and, while most of the public either wasn't aware or concerned or both, he defended his music whenever he had a chance. His players, incidentally, were considered avant-garde dressers. A member of the Lawrence Welk band later told a writer that when the two bands crossed each other's path, you quickly knew Kenton players.

"Kenton, Woody Herman and some other progressive bands tended to look rather seedy when they got off the bus. Hadn't shaved, coats and pants rumpled. Maybe it was the image they wanted... we were considered the goody two-shoe bands and they were the roustabouts," he said with a laugh.

Kenton suffered the consequences of such defiance. His stubborn resistance brought periods of financial ruin and bankruptcy. Yet, he hired some of the top players of the day at attractive salaries and played concerts that some called "noise" and he tried to ignore gigs where dance music was necessary. On the other hand, few would disagree that Kenton's dance band played some excellent arrangements with melody and rhythm to entice and glide people on the dance floor. He even did some novelty numbers that actually were funny (musicians have difficulty with humor; too much inside bandstand humor confused listeners.)

His Balboa Beach band of the 1940s brought young California couples to the shores of the Pacific to "swing and sway" to his own creation called *Artistry in Rhythm* and lush renditions of such standards as *Autumn in New York* and *September Song* where he ordered the whole band to sing a couple of verses in unison for a recording. He loved the feedback although the band thought it schlocky. He did it again with sidemen singing a sentimental number called *Laura*. Again, it was a hit.

joe Enroughty leading his Royal Virginian Orchestra
Photo courtesy of Joe Enroughty

But the band could certainly swing in a conventional way, too. Arrangers like Pete Rugolo and others gave him well-crafted, up-tempo numbers like *And Her Tears Flowed Like Wine* and *Tampico* with singer June Christy and a smooth number called *Dynaflow* named after the famous Buick automatic drive of the day. Most fans liked the Kenton band the way it was. But Stan continued to experiment which caused even loyal fans to be exasperated. One music critic called Kenton music "appallingly pretentious pap." Others were more severe.

He didn't relent and he wasn't contrite either. An illness took him off the road for three years or so and when he returned he basically turned his back on leading a dance band. He added strings, hired very avant garde composers like Bob Graettinger and others and took his music into what he called *Innovations in Modern Music*. There wasn't much that was danceable. He left his meat and potatoes and didn't look back.

I thought he was courageous at the time. The leader of our society band thought it was suicide and others offered similar sentiments. I remember a

The Pier Ballroom   Photo courtesy of Buckeye Lake (OH) Museum

letter to *Downbeat* where a reader took Kenton to task for ruining the business for others. Stan must have read the letter. In his *Downbeat* piece shortly after he returned to the business in 1950 he said: "Everybody can blame Woody Herman, Dizzy Gillespie and me for ruining the dance band business and I'll agree with them. Sure, we ruined it. We ruined it because we were bound and determined to play the kind of music we wanted to play. What we wanted to play wasn't dance music, but despite this, the agents and promoters insisted on handling us just as they would handle a dance band."

He was out of step with the public and the band business, clearly was far too musically rebellious for people who didn't understand the product. If it said dance band and it had a theme song… that's what it must have been, right? Yet promoters and ballroom owners who should have known better… didn't. Most of the public liked music to dance to, hum along with and enjoy listening to… they weren't with Stan and his music which promoters called "ahead of his time."

I was fortunate enough to play with a band that knew exactly the kind of crowds they played for and their purpose in such entertainment. They were, of course, the territorial bands where most big bands evolved. Names like Glenn Miller, Tommy and Jimmy Dorsey, Gene Krupa, Claude Thornhill and hundreds of other celebrity players started in territorial bands. It was the minor leagues but it frequently had more permanence than the major touring league. Even then, we were forced to play sets of square dance music, even some polkas! Big band musicians, we told ourselves, DIDN'T play such music and several of us protested one night. A fellow sideman and I put our disagreement into action and we refused to play the square dance set. The leader played the drums and the band went ahead without us. The leader, Dick Trimble, a rough talking guy with a gentle streak, didn't shout at us. But after the gig he let us know with firmness and conviction that such a protest wouldn't happen again. "We play requests and we play what the audience wants. If you can't do that, better find some other band," he growled at me.

The big band days have been described as lasting about a decade with a few years on either side of the 1940s. It was fueled by the tensions and hysteria of World War II, a great amount of dreamy and hopeful music and bandleaders struggling to keep groups together as the draft took their players into the service. Glenn Miller, who volunteered to join the military although he was over the draft age, was the towering musical figure of the era because he sensed the need for patriotism, music with strong melody and the need to appeal to ordinary people doing extraordinary things.

Said Ronald Reagan, host of the Swinging Singing Big Band Years Video of 1950: "By 1950, bandsmen began settling down, people were home watching television and entertainment had changed. But swing music was and continues to be the universal language that is our best hope of one day changing the world with harmony that will bring us together…"

It hasn't happened yet… but you can't blame the music or musicians. Yet while the music continues, the big band era and the dancing it spawned remain in a death spiral of economics, changing entertainment and changing demographics. Howard Schneider, who has led the Jan Garber band for years, told the *Garber Gabbings Newsletter* "The older folks who like to dance to our kind of music are dying off." The younger generation which didn't grow up with swing and dance music is unaware of the famous orchestras of the past and their music. Says Schneider: "It begins to appear that only the biggest names in the dance band business will ultimately survive." Most of us hope he's wrong.

1 Lee, Dr. William F., American Big Bands, Hal Leonard, 2005
2 www.themix.com/performer/350613/ba-rolfe

Territorial Dance Bands

America's Unsung Music Makers

They were the bands you danced to and the musicians you talked to as you glided by the bandstand on the soft hardwood floor. You usually knew some of the players. Maybe the leader. He may have sold you an insurance policy or perhaps he came out to unplug your drains. That's what it was like in a territorial band anywhere in America from the early 1900s to today. Musicians worked day jobs to exist and spent weekends, holidays and vacations enjoying their first love; playing gigs in big bands helping people enjoy their evenings. They were paid from $10 to $100 an evening generally; sometimes less, sometimes more.

America was changing too. The Louisville Slugger baseball bat was introduced, the Coca Cola company was formed and Buddy Boldin's Original Jazz Orchestra was playing the streets and amusement parks in New Orleans. George Eastman had developed the famous box camera which recorded some of the early scenes of the country and its jazz roots.

But it would take 27 years before what music historians claimed was the first dance orchestra would be recognized. Wilbur C. Sweatman, a self-taught musician who was able to play three instruments at once, put together an orchestra which played Chicago's Pekin Theater in 1912.

Sweatman was a story of musical success at a time when blacks found little or no opportunities in any part of the country. He toured with circus bands in the 1890s before he organized his own group in Minneapolis, MN in 1902. He made his first recording a year later for a local music store which included what is considered the first recorded version of Scott Joplin's famous "Maple Leaf Rag."

He moved to Chicago in 1908 and became bandleader at the Grand Theatre where he attracted attention as the "Sensational Swet." A relationship with Joplin continued and later in life was so close, the famous black songwriter named Sweatman the executor of his estate including many unpublished songs. An Indiana newspaper described Sweatman as diminutive in stature but with "a style and grace of manner in all of his executions that is at once convincing, and the soulfulness of expression that he blends into his tones is something wonderful. His first number was a medley of popular airs and 'rags' and had everybody shuffling their pedal extremities before it was half over.'"

San Francisco was still rebuilding from the devastating 1906 earthquake when Art Hickman and his band, who played in the St. Francis Hotel in the city, came up with special arrangements and introduced the touring big band. A baseball fan, Art followed the San Francisco Seals baseball club and when manager Del Howard took the team to Sonoma County for spring training the bandleader approached club ownership with a novel idea; why not sponsor a series of dances to relieve the boredom at the camp? Howard liked the idea and Hickman found new gigs playing for baseball players and their wives and girl friends. Like so many connections, the celebrated Florenz Ziegfeld of Follies' fame happened to catch the Hickman band at the spring camp—he also was a baseball fan—and invited the group to NYC to play the Biltmore and the Ziegfeld Roof.

Territorial bands got their start in the Jazz Age playing for friends, neighbors and family and rehearsing continually. *Variety Magazine*, the bible for musicians, singers and booking agents in the 1920s and later, reported in 1924 that there were 900 dance orchestras representing 7,200 musicians. They also reported that some leaders recognized their name value at the same time. Paul Whiteman, who was called the "King of Jazz," had 68 orchestras in his name, 11 of them in New York. Jack Jenny of Mason City, IA, knew he wanted such a life. He started on the trumpet at 8 but switched to the trombone when he entered Cedar Rapids High School. At 18, he was good enough to get an audition with the popular Austin Wylie band when it came through Iowa and he was selected to join the band where he got to know a young Artie Shaw in the sax section.

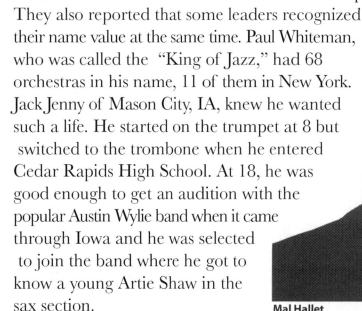

Mal Hallet

Photo courtesy of Lou DiSario

Within six years he had jumped to Mal Hallett's band and spent a couple of years with legendary Isham Jones playing with another player of later fame, Woody Herman, and he was a section mate with the great trombonist Jack Teagarden. The Depression, meantime, took its toll among musicians as it did many other fields of employment. In 1933, half of the bands working in 1924 were out of business and some of the musicians were stranded in cities and towns throughout the country and surviving on soup kitchens. In the midwest, Serl Frank Hutton organized the National Orchestra Service (NOS) to book territory bands throughout the Great Plains and other regions. NOS was based at Omaha National Bank Building, Downtown Omaha, and represented Glenn Miller styled bands that featured 12 to 15 pieces. It continued through the Depression but folded in early 1960.

In 1938, Jack launched his own band which soon failed and he married Kay Thompson who had her own group at the time. The marriage failed too. He appeared in two movies, *Syncopation* and *Stage Door Canteen* during the war years. He took over the Bobby Byrne band when the leader enlisted in the military service. Jack also served in the military for a year before being discharged for poor health. An Iowa Public Television's Jazz feature says that Jack's time with Artie Shaw was perhaps his "finest hour publicly in a 1941 recording of 'Stardust.' The version is still heard today led by the strong trumpet of Billy Butterfield, but Jack Jenny's half chorus fits in nicely after Shaw's solo."[1] His touring took him to Hollywood where he did the Dick Haymes radio show, *Something for the Boys*, as the war was ending. He suffered an appendectomy in Hollywood and died at the early age of 35. His story was too common among young musicians, primarily from the east and Midwest, who sacrificed health and welfare to gain recognition in the sun and fun of the west coast.

Jack got his beginning in territory work but was determined to reach higher. You had to have excellent tools to earn the money touring musicians got. College degrees weren't necessary but because ambitious bandleaders marketed their bands for movies and radio as well of one nighters, you had to be a reader, preferably a "sight reader" someone who could "read" a chart and play it right away. Amazingly, a number of musicians at the territorial as well as the touring levels were non-readers. Well known tenor saxophonist Vito Musso who worked with the Woody Herman and Stan Kenton bands and soloed with both, was among the talented but limited musicians of the day. Like many, they played by "ear" listening to numbers played by others or on the piano and then let their mind store the music. Pianist Errol Garner and celebrated drummers like Gene Krupa and

Glen Miller
Photo courtesy of Lou DiSario

Buddy Rich were among the legions who played without the benefit of understanding notes on paper. Their recall was extraordinary. It was a gift, musical friends said, and many agree.

Of course, you needed talent. One of the saddest things I remember as a musician was listen to a person playing an instrument but not "feeling" the music. No vibrado, no tonal quality and frequently only a knowledge of what was on the sheet of music. Careers were lost because of such a lack of emotion in playing the music. It helped, obviously, if you were versatile enough to play other instruments and do what was called "doubling."

You didn't find touring bandleaders advertising for personnel... they relied for decades on passing the word out and connecting with respected musicians in their own bands or others.

Glenn Miller and Benny Goodman, two of the country's top touring bands, not only demanded auditions to join their groups, they insisted on quality as it applied to the sections of their bands. A player who lacked tonal quality (either no vibrato or too much) could lose the spot whether in rehearsal or on the job.

Benny was known to use his so-called "ray" (an icy stare) to get a person to leave the stage and sometimes the band. Playing demanded excellence nightly to a number of leaders. According to Benny, there was good reason for perfection every performance. He told Christopher Popa (www.bigbandlibrary.com) bandleading resembled "a slippery cake of ice. Standing still for a moment results in a case of cold feet. Sit down even for a moment and the competition may freeze you out. Bask for an aimless hour in the sunshine of your glory and that ice paradise melts right out from under you."

Glenn also had high standards during his life with both the civilian and military Miller bands and saxophonist Dick Gerhart, who spent 20 years with the orchestra and five years as its leader, felt the same pressure. At his death in 2006, Dick had spent 7,000 nights on the road working 50 weeks a year continuing the Miller sound and insisting on the integrity of the music that made it the most popular dance band ever.

Although the big band craze continued to excite dancers and musicians, times were still tough in early 1940 and continued during the war years. Unions restricted the fees of agents and managers in an attempt to protect local or territorial musicians from touring groups which frequently paid two to five times more and forced the name bands to cut their need for sidemen. The explosion of commercial free radio and recordings added more pressure on employing live bands. In a growing number of smaller communities where a family had eked out a living running a ballroom, many closed during the week and later permanently.

Making matters far worse, the American Federation of Musicians (AFM) led by a man many musicians and business people felt was a martinet, James Petrillo, called for a strike in 1942-43 and later in 1948. Coupled with technical advancements in amplification which introduced the electric guitar and overnight interest in singers and a popular radio show on Saturday nights called *Your Hit Parade*, big band popularity faded. Ironically, the singers on *Your Hit Parade* radio show were exempt from the ban. Finding work, therefore, was nearly impossible unless you had solid connections with people in the band or the leader.

Think about a saxophone player who auditioned for Guy Lombardo and had to learn the use of very strong vibrato. On the other hand, imagine what a saxophone player had to do to join composer/arranger/ bandleader Billy May back in the 1950s when he discovered he had to conquer the technique of "slurping" in unison with four other players. Creating a sliding scale sound with four to five saxophone players took continued practice to play in unison and, although they played on the road nightly, it still required constant work to reach the standard Billy wanted. Add the rigors of the road, getting your clothes laundered in new towns and cities and grabbing a bite to eat when you could and touring became the challenge that got older as you aged. Bassist Rollie Bundock who traveled with Glenn Miller and Les Brown among others once told me: "When we went on the road everything became a blur. Night after night on and off the bus. I remember once I got back home and I had 12 pieces of laundry that followed me. I tried to see my folks at least three or four times a year but I would get home for just a few hours and then it would be off to Boston or New York or wherever we were playing and the bus was leaving."

Said my friend Lou DiSario, a Philadelphian who toured for several years with the Harmonicats as a singer, dancer and emcee: "Most people who came to see us never realized the sacrifices and demands touring musicians faced. We were clean shaven, mustaches trimmed and we had fresh or nearly fresh clothes every performance. We had to perform at our best every time out regardless of how we felt. I watched guy and girl singers get off buses groggy from lack of sleep for days as they tried to meet a booker's impossible schedule that put them in Chicago one night, Cincinnati or Cleveland the next, followed by Atlanta the third night and then return to Ohio to play a college prom and leave the gig right away to get to New York City and we're talking two-lane highways and 50 mile an hour speed laws. Cold food, a little too much alcohol to numb aches and pains and total lack of sleep took its toll on everyone."

Most people who came to see us never realized the sacrifices and demands touring musicians faced.

Lou became a territorial player when he realized the loss of income traveling as well as the loss of sleep were sacrifices that hurt physically and financially. He liked the fact he could sleep in his own bed, he smiled. And he said he was willing to get off the road when he found a way to continue what he loved; performing near home. "This wasn't a business to me… it was a hobby that takes devotion and love with little thought of what you'd get besides applause… you know it was not going to pay your bills."

You weren't always sure the mood of the touring band leader when you showed up to work as an emcee, Lou recalled. "I worked years at Hamid's Pier Ballroom and the house band was Ed Morgan which was easy. The touring bandleaders were a different matter. I played recorded music during short breaks. At the Steel Pier, the breaks were 15 to 20 minutes for major bands although some came in and set their own rules, infuriating the ballroom owners. They would take half hour interludes and we'd play recorded music and the ticket prices were $4 or more which was big money in the late 1930s and early '40s. Harry James was great to work with… Glenn Miller wasn't. I had to introduce his numbers and he simply didn't tell me. It was embarrassing at times," Lou said.[2]

Most musicians, whether they're leaders or sidemen, say the money was hardly the inducement to stay in the music business whether playing in a territorial or touring band. It's too demanding and the pay is too uneven to make it your only income and survive. "If you don't truly love it, such work can take a lot out of you," says Gary Greenfelder, a trumpet player and leader of a popular Detroit big band called *OneBeatBack*. "For me, all this is very exciting and there are plenty of opportunities to have a lot of fun doing what we love to do!" One of the more difficult tasks is understanding the crowd in front of you, he told me. Misread that and you probably won't be invited back. Worse, word of mouth can cause others not to book you either. "You don't show up to play a concert with only dance numbers and you better not show up at a dance with lengthy concert numbers."

OneBeatBack has played governor's galas, the Detroit Yacht Club, church vespers, dinner parties and wedding receptions and several years ago when Chrysler was a major auto company it played the company's Top Ten Road Rally. Yet, the band is just as comfortable playing the Hamburg Family Fun Fest in Hamburg Township, MI. Simply put, he said, "you love to play and you love to play for people."[3]

It took physical endurance and energy every day, many sidemen said of their ordeals on the road, and it had its hilarious moments as well as its low spots.

In the 1920s and '30s, Eddie Condon in his *Scrapbook* described how he got a gig on a cruise ship. "I thought I could cut it and it would be a gas! The cruise ship was going to Argentina and I signed on to play piano. I'm a good sailor but a bad piano player. I could only play in one key so the entire band had to play four times a day in the key of F for 14,000 miles." It must have been a grueling cruise on the band although I doubt the guests figured it out unless they played piano.[4]

Chuz Alfred, who toured with big bands and small combos for a number of years, later wrote about his feelings as he made the decision to leave the road.

"The guys were coming 'an'goin'… I didn't hang out that much or get to know them that well. It was a totally different groove than the one I had been used to earlier. I didn't like to sit down while playing and I could not get used to having to strain to see the charts under lights that could be candle power or bright. Then you'd pack it up and move on after just about every gig.

Chuz Alfred   Photo courtesy of Chuz Alfred

It left me numb just sort of floating around."⁵

Exactly what has been the role of the territorial band?

Wikipedia provides one answer. They were generally dance bands that played in specific states or regions of the country — the east, the south, midwest, southwest and far west — and barnstormed at particular times of the year. They were hometown bands that played the VFW, Elks Lodges, FOE, hotel ballrooms for any number of local groups and they were known for their dance book and danceable beats. They were an outlet for young and middle aged couples like my parents to socialize, meet members of the opposite sex, have fun dancing and listening to stock charts of Tin Pan Alley music that were advertised as the rage in New York City, San Francisco, Chicago or elsewhere.

Young, talented musicians talked at length about their road dreams every time a touring major band made an appearance close by. Listen to saxophonist Paul Kumler, an experienced territorial musician who played with a number of bands in Central Ohio including Dick Trimble's society band: "We took our sound very seriously. Some bands really never practiced that much. They just played their gigs and probably didn't get together until the next week. Trimble believed in practice." Drummer Kenny Carpenter remembered rehearsals with the Trimble band "as every day work for an hour or more. Dick would mark the sheet music in the sax section so they would all breathe at the same time. The sound? It was out of sight!"

Paul remembered the excitement and dejection that could accompany getting a chance to play with major bands. An excellent clarinetist and saxophone player, Dick was eager to get a chance to show his abilities, Paul said. He never lost his enthusiasm. "Dick got a call I remember that a major touring band — Sam Donahue maybe, I'm not sure — was going to be at nearby Buckeye Lake that night and they needed an alto saxophonist. Dick was already out the door with his sax and on his motorcycle heading to the lake. When he got there several hours before the gig, he was told they already had filled the chair. They thanked him for his promptness. He didn't talk about it much but he always hoped there would be another time. Touring gigs came and went that fast in those days."⁶

Such freelancing was always a sign of recognition to territorial players but it was seen differently by nationally known bandleaders. Frank Galime, an accomplished symphonic and big band trumpet player who played in major groups from New York to Florida, remembered when he joined the Warren Covington band as a replacement at a gig in Utica, NY. Prior to the dance, Covington told him to refrain from waving at people or talking to locals. "He told me that when people pay a higher amount to see a touring group like his they don't like the fact that locals are on the stand which says that the band isn't a touring group. We don't want people thinking we're a pickup band. But even warning me about doing anything like shaking hands with the trumpet player sitting next to me didn't help much. So when I had an impromptu solo and stood up to play, somebody on the floor shouted 'there's Frank playing with the band… good work, Frank!' Covington stared at me for several minutes but said nothing. Some things you simply can't control," Frank said with a smile.[7]

I saw the Covington band in Ohio and it was a good sounding group with musicians who gave good performances and solos. Warren was asked once by *BigBandLibrary.com*'s interviewer Christopher Popa where he got the interest to lead his own band. Covington told Popa "Well the germ of that had been put into my head by Horace Heidt. In '41, '42 and '43 I was with Heidt and he wanted to get and own three places. He wanted to… set me up with a band, Frankie Carle and a band and him. He did buy the Casino Gardens down in Santa Monica, he wanted to buy the Graystone Manor in Detroit and he wanted to buy the Glen Island Casino in New Rochelle, NY which was owned by the state."

Lou DiSario- Singer, Entertainer　　　Photo courtesy of Lou DiSario

Complicated legal battles in the industry ended the dream.

But it never ended Warren's love of the music business. "I mean this is my life, and I treat every performance as if it was for the worldwide television. Cause I love it. I'm very fussy. I like class. I like a classy band. I like a classy act and I like it diversified," he told Popa. He made good on his promise the night I saw him.

Occasionally leaders had instant vacancies with little hope of finding replacements in time. In the 1960s, the Duke Ellington Orchestra was on a swing through the southwest to play the Las Vegas Desert Inn. Trombonist Milt Bernhart remembers he was working in Vegas too and wanted to hear the Duke. He got to the Desert Inn at intermission and was told that two of Duke's trumpet players had been busted on drug charges and no one knew whether they would perform in the second half of the program. But Milt hung around curious about how the Ellington band would finish the gig down two trumpet players. He got his answer moments later when Duke and others returned to the bandstand and began the second half… without the entire four man trumpet section!

Said Milt: "Ellington walked on stage to tumultuous applause, smiled and began to play… and he gave no sign whatsoever that he noticed the four empty chairs in the top row. I'll never forget it… I was absolutely floored and I've never gotten over it. All of the music — solos, of course, but full-band passages… all of it, every note — was pure Ellington… Maybe as good as I've heard too! I swear I heard trumpets. I know Duke heard them. He never looked so happy!"[8]

Major bandleaders who needed income and one nighters to keep their groups working encountered insurmountable obstacles during World War II. The demand for dance bands leaped just as draft boards began calling up many young, draft-eligible musicians into the military services. Pearl Harbor brought a rush of patriotism as young men lined up to volunteer and others went home to wait for their Selective Service orders. Either way, it was an impossible mission for leaders to keep personnel let alone book gigs.

The Japanese attack on the Hawaiian Islands still came as a shock to most Americans including military and civilian authorities. By the evening of Dec. 7, 1941, all dances on the islands and along the west coast of the United States had been cancelled because of curfews and blackouts. A midnight curfew went into effect that day and it continued during the war years forcing organizations to start dances early. Furthermore, you didn't end a public performance with "Goodnight Irene" either. It was required that all formal engagements finish with the playing of the *Star Spangled Banner*.

Within months, rationing added new restrictions and bands and their leaders felt the pain as did the public. In 1942, there were 800 ballrooms and amusement parks scattered throughout America but getting to them was challenging. Roads were in disrepair and gas and tires were rationed.

Worse, the United States was still a racially divided country. Here's what Ed Gabel said about how the Stan Kenton band dealt with one such incident. The band wanted to stay at the Bakersfield Inn on Highway 99 in California. "When we entered the dining room the manager politely turned us away telling Stan he was sorry but Negroes were not permitted in the dining room. Bob Gioga, who was our group leader, tried telling the manager that Karl (a black musician from the Los Angeles Musicians Union who joined the tour during the war years) was Cuban. The hotel manager didn't accept that; he feared offending other guests and wouldn't buy Gioga's story. We turned to leave in frustration when the manager made a suggestion. If we wished, he was willing to set up a table in the kitchen where we could be served. I could understand his reason; we were potential customers and business is business. There was nothing left to do, so we took a vote and the ayes won. Reflecting back 50 years, I wonder if it was the right decision."[9]

Some bands sought distinctive images that leaders and their agents actively promoted. Even in those pre-marketing survey days bandleaders were trying to find successful devices or sounds that grew audiences. Glenn Miller was by far the most successful leader and he worked at it day and night. He made sure that the band had recorded his most recent songs before the group went on the road. He actively cultivated fan clubs (which some leaders disdained) among the chooches (fans) and he even irritated his best soloists by urging them to play the same solo night after night. "That's what really made me want to leave the band." Billy May told me. "Solos were to be creative expression not repetitious phrases and I'm sure Glenn knew that but he also knew that people liked to hear what they had on their records and in jukeboxes."

Gimmicks could also create a band's sound. Shep Fields became popular in the 1930s thanks to his wife blowing bubbles into her soda through a straw at a soda shop. He used the sound but held a contest to see if fans in Chicago could name his new band. The term "rippling rhythm" was popular among Chicago's Palmer House listeners. The band's title? Shep Fields and his "Rippling Rhythm Orchestra." The band remained a popular old-fashioned ballroom orchestra until it disbanded in 1953 when Shep went to work in Houston, TX as a disc jockey.

Dick Jurgens and His Orchestra at the Palladium, CA   Photo courtesy of wikipedi.org

Alex Bartha
Photo courtesy of Lou DiSario

Other bands, like the popular west coast Dick Jurgens orchestra, was concerned about the looks of his organization. Dick was a stickler for shoes shined, proper uniforms and haircuts. His band, said some of his musicians and their wives, was a family, a group of people who tried to distance themselves from the image associated with some bands. Dick repaid them, too. He organized his tours so that the band would be in preferred resort locations over long holiday periods and invited them to bring along their wives and families. You didn't drink or do drugs on the Jurgens band a few of his sidemen told entertainment reporters. While Dick eventually gained a national name and played Chicago, Denver and elsewhere, to Californians he was a territorial band based at the Hotel Claremont just outside San Francisco. His theme song *Daydreams*, which was first recorded Aug. 19, 1939, was the opener for many radio remotes that began like a travelog:

"Once again, from out of the west, the beauty spot of California – the world famous Guard Room of the Hotel Claremont, high atop the Oakland/Berkeley Hills, overlooking San Francisco Bay, just a few minutes drive from the city of the Golden Gate and around the nation, the music of Dick Jurgens and his Orchestra."

Miller's patriotism undoubtedly influenced many. But his trombone playing was a different story. He had his detractors who felt he didn't have the range or quality of a Tommy Dorsey or Jack Teagarden. The criticism persisted which bothered Glenn who was so sensitive to the grumblings he was said to frequently refuse take a solo in impromptu sessions when in the company of Dorsey and Teagarden or others. Yet, all agreed that his management ability, discipline and arranging skills were admired by friends as well as competitors. "Whether you liked him or not, he was, without a doubt, a tremendous talent at the time," said Lou DiSario.

Later biographers let readers know that Tommy Dorsey's secret technique in playing was his breath control. Dorsey, it seems, had a tiny hole in his mouth which allowed air in without it being seen. His father, "Pop," taught him how to use his physical difference to give him the quick breath that other players didn't have.

Unlike some bandleaders, Glenn could set a dance beat easily and he understood what good foxtrot rhythm was. His mixture of melodic, dreamy dance music and a few up-tempo or novelty numbers was very popular, too. While a number of bandleaders didn't dance, Glenn danced with his wife Helen occasionally. "He knew how we felt about our partner and that made him special," said any number of dancers who heard and loved Miller.

Idiosyncrasies abounded among the musicians of the era. Artie Shaw was convinced he was a better clarinetist than his friend and friendly rival Benny Goodman and he said so when pressed. He normally let people know that he was self taught, Goodman was classically trained.

Bob Crosby came to music thanks to brother Bing. Bob's connections gave him the opportunity to start a Dixieland band, called the Bobcats, which created its own popularity. His group produced two excellent Dixie hits, *South Rampart Street Parade* and *Big Noise from Winnetka,* and his looks, the Crosby name and personality gave him roles in some 20 feature films over 40 years in Hollywood.

But each bandleader and sideman — almost exclusively all men — had to live with the day-to-day tension of draft boards looking for eligible candidates to fill higher and higher military quotas from the War Department.

Pianist Joe Bushkin entered the service in '42. Blue Barron was drafted into the army airbourne of all branches to serve while Tommy Ryan took over his band. Bobby Byrne accepted a commission in the Army Air Force, Dick Jurgens went into the Marines and formed a band in the Pacific Theater, Rudy Vallee enlisted in the Coast Guard, Claude Thornhill went into the navy and requested combat duty, Eddie Duchin and Orrin Tucker entered the navy and Tex Beneke, who was with the Miller band its last civilian performance at Central Theater, Passaic, NJ, didn't enter the service until he was drafted months later. He was inducted into the navy and spent his service time leading a band in land-locked Oklahoma. Ray Anthony and Doc Severinsen were both drafted and trumpeter Clyde McCoy, realizing that trying to continue to work as a civilian musician during war years was useless, talked his whole band into joining as a group.

Duchin, a pharmacist turned pianist and bandleader, became an overnight sensation at Manhattan nightclubs thanks to radio remotes. A self-taught pianist, he enlisted in the navy and served as a combat officer. After the war, he couldn't recapture his pre-war popularity and, at 41, he died of leukemia. Hollywood capitalized on his dashing but tragic life in the movie *The Eddie Duchin Story.*

Meanwhile, the stateside public was harshly critical of men — especially celebrities —who didn't serve in the defense of the country. By 1942 the war's impact in the Pacific among the valiant soldiers, sailors and marines battling a superior and ruthless Japanese army, navy and air force and the push to build a large allied military might to confront Germany and Italy unsettled communities across the country. Conscientious objectors were singled out in towns and communities and even banned from a few establishments by large signs that told them they weren't welcomed. The same treatment applied to those deemed unfit for service. Bandleaders Harry James, Benny Goodman and Kay Kyser were rejected for physical handicaps and felt the public humiliation although they tried to serve. All three voluntarily took their bands to any number of army, navy and air force USO dances and patriotic events to demonstrate their commitment to the war effort and frequently took part in war bond programs.

Kyser's case was an example of how a bandleader's notoriety could test the "selectivity" of the national system. Kay was nearly beyond the Selective Service age limit of 38 when his draft board in Rocky Mount, NC put him on the induction list. Although considered nearly blind without glasses and hampered by a trick knee, he had never appealed or ask for a deferment but the Selective Service system was well aware of what the popular bandleader had contributed as a civilian to the military cause. He and his band outperformed all other entertainers by putting on 1,100 performances in over 300 camps and, in addition, he sold $95 millions in war bonds.

Said the Ol' Professor as he pondered what might happen: "This puts me on a real spot. If ah pass the physical and they give me a band job, people will all say ah've got a soft touch. If ah don't, they'll swear it was a put-up job. Ah hope they give me a job fighting." His 4-F classification probably helped the war effort!

Big bands, however, never lost their appeal during the war years. Veteran disc jockey and big band aficionado David Miller told me you could see the enthusiasm when you entered the ballroom in the 1940s. "I always remember a photo of college kids at a Stan Kenton dance date. The guys are gathered around the bandstand watching and listening intently. Their dates are with them but look as though they'd rather be dancing. I think it was a definite guy-girl thing. Both liked to dance, but it was the guys who knew the musicians and could name every instrumental after the first two bars. It's the same today. Ninety

Ninety percent of my triva contestants are male, while women call in to request a romantic tune they danced to in high school.

percent of my trivia contestants are male, while women call in to request a romantic tune they danced to in high school."[10]

There was a different atmosphere, however, when the band was local as compared to a touring, nationally known orchestra. There tended to be less dancing and more watching and listening when a major group was on the bandstand. People came to dance to local groups, I found. And leaders of the bands I played with responded by playing far more dance tunes.

Touring big bands had their own difficulties when they showed up to play. Jack Sandmeier, now a member of Atlanta's Sentimental Journey Orchestra, remembers his days when he traveled as a bandboy and then a road manager with Stan Kenton. "Stan's contracts called for a grand piano tuned at A440 pitch. Most of the time the promoters would comply, however when you do 50 weeks a year on the road, there were always those jobs that were dubious, with contractual complaints. We were playing an old ballroom someplace and an upright spinet piano was supplied. Worse yet, there were two keys that didn't work. So through the whole gig, Stan kept playing those two keys which would crack the audience up. Finally at the end of the gig, while the band was playing the ending theme, Stan took out a matchbook, lit the book with one match, opened the top of the piano, and threw it in, then acted as if it was going to blow up. The audience loved it."

Sweet touring bands were very popular and it was the reason they enjoyed real success when they went on the road. Bands like Sammy Kaye, Blue Barron, Lombardo, Eddy Howard, Henry Busse, Russ Carlyle, Lawrence Welk, Paul Whiteman, Jerry Gray, Jan Garber, Ralph Flanagan, Carmen Cavallaro, Charley Spivak, Glen Gray and others had strong

Chick Webb
Photo courtesy of wikipedia.org

appeal in ballrooms everywhere. Lombardo, one of the most successful of the distinctive sweet bands, left Chicago for the Roosevelt Room in New York City in 1929 and a 47 year old contract that made him and the song "Auld Lang Syne" famous every New Year's Eve via radio. Meanwhile, he traveled 60,000 miles a year playing colleges and small towns when he wasn't racing his speedboats.

The select group of touring bands that worked through agencies and gained notoriety were a small part of the bands traveling and playing ballrooms city to city. I've included those I found reviewing the radio remotes prepared by Cra-bapple Sound of Old Time Radio and Wikipedia's article on Big Band Remotes.[11]

Black bands were slowly gaining acceptance outside the cities where they had roots and local support. When the dimuitive drummer Chick Webb, ravaged by tuberculosis of the spine but driven by ambition to have the best band in the 1930s, showed up outside New York City at an country club in New Hartford, NY, to play a high school prom, the band raised eyebrows. New York state had long since been integrated but upstate like so many other places in the country wasn't. A territory band determined to have the luster of Benny Goodman, Harry James, Glenn Miller and black counterparts like Fletcher Henderson, Duke Ellington, and everybody's favorite Jimmy Lunceford, Chick was positioning himself to use gigs outside the city to get more notoriety. He was well-established in the city at places like the Apollo, the Savoy and the Cotton Club where he had been the "house" band and won virtually every battle of the bands held but his promoters believed he needed more exposure. A young singer named Ella Fitzgerald was with the band direct from her smash hit *A-Tisket, A-Tasket*. It was spring, 1939, and Ozzie Nelson was opening at Russells Danceland on Sylvan Beach on the shores of Oneida Lake. But black bands like Chick's were still a novelty in some regions of the country. Upstaters heard black bands on the radio, saw photos of such groups but they hadn't been live in the area. When the touring sedan pulled up in front of the Yahnundasis Country Club on the circular driveway to play a high school dance and a few musicians got out they were waved to "go around to the back." The inference was help entered through the rear door. But Chick, Ella and the band put on a typical show of dance music and the Lindy Hop, the rage in New York City at the time. Sadly, Chick died of his disease within a few months and Ella took over the Webb band which became *Ella Fitzgerald and her Famous Orchestra.*

Success was illusive for any number of talented musicians working on the edge of the exclusive bands and leaders. Billy May, for example, spent years playing on such famous bands as Glenn Miller—he left Miller pre-World War II because of disagreements with Glenn—and introducing arrangements that gave fame to friends. It was Billy who created a Ray Noble piece that became Charley Barnet's major hit "Cherokee." It was also Billy who ended up rewriting the whole Barnet book of nearly 100 or more charts when Charley's music burned up in the Palomar Theater fire, October, 1938.

May showed his versatility when he went to work for Paul Weston, musical director of the newly organized Capitol Records Co, and ghost arranged for him. He worked with singers like Bing Crosby, Frank Sinatra—he did the 'Come Dance With Me' and 'Come Swing With Me' series with Frank—and others.

Billy demonstrated his incredible talent at Capitol when he spent 10 years producing a series of children's story/song records. One that was popular was the kitty cat song *I Tawt I Taw A Putty Tat*.

In the mid 1950s, Billy decided to capitalize on the success he was generating by creating a distinctive sound for the sax section called "slurping" (all the saxophones controlling their breathing to go up and down the scales in unison). He put together his first big band, unfortunately, when ballrooms and larger groups were going out of business. He kept his group together for about two years but gave it up because of his irritation playing one nighters and the difficulties of marketing the band. He left the circuit and returned to the studio to help Sinatra put together a successful album called *Come Fly With Me*.

Most major bandleaders in the 1930s and '40s were territorial musicians in their teens when they started. In the east, a prominent territory band was Art Bronson's Bostonians, in New York fans came out when the Savoy Sultans or Chick Webb was on the bandstand at The Savoy or the Cotton Club, Mal Hallett was a popular New England band and Jimmy Lunceford could excite a crowd of dancers in Buffalo. Pianist Claude Thornhill was one of the few with classical training (Cincinnati Conservatory and the Curtis Institute of Philadelphia) from Terra Haute, IN when he auditioned and was hired by Austin Wylie, a popular territorial band based in Cleveland. He became close friends with Wylie's clarinetist Artie Shaw, a self-taught player, and Vaughn Monroe, a trumpet player who went on to lead a very successful band as a singer.

The big band could be any number of things depending upon the arrangements. Benny Goodman's western tour was quite successful when he used Fletcher Henderson's swing charts which bystanders said ignited the crowds and propelled Benny on his way back to the east coast. Unlike Dixieland bands that were pick up groups of ukele or guitar, clarinet, trumpet, trombone, drums, bass or tuba and piano, big bands were usually eight to as many as twenty musicians playing scripted arrangements and they could be loud depending upon the acoustics of the hall, ballroom or club. The amazing thing looking at some of the very well known dancing spots was how large bands squeezed into tiny bandshells and how smaller groups could produce such a large sound without amplification.

Said Eddie Condon, a well known jazz guitarist and club owner in the city: "Every Kenton record sounds to me as though Stan signed on three hundred men for the date and they were all on time. Music of his school, in my opinion, ought only to be played close to elephants and listened to only by clowns."

Yet, he added with a smile, "it's a real accomplishment to take that many men and make them sound ruly."[12]

Eddie liked small groupings of particular instruments which fit comfortably in small clubs or rooms in larger buildings. It was the obvious antithesis to what big bands created and their fans enjoyed. Big band music was swing, a type of music that could be heard from one end of the ballroom to the other and contained a solid beat. The big band arrangement followed a standard pattern; melody played by the entire band in unison or harmony, soloists improvising from the song's melody style and chord progression and the melody restated in different setting. The touring big bands grew quickly to fill the demand from large halls and ballrooms that were anxious to capture the national dancing scene in their own communities and coast to coast radio remotes which promoted such excitement. Since the microphone wasn't in existence until 1935, brassy big bands with drummers sporting large bass drums were popular.

Territory bands evolved because national booking agents ignored the

Aragon Ballroom   Photo courtesy of James Ronan Collection IA

vast midlands of the country. Touring bands were busy scheduling the top talent in well known city sites like the Aragon Ballroom in Chicago, the Palladium in Hollywood, the Cotton Club in New York City and others. Territory bands used stock arrangements available from music companies although a few were creative enough to arrange some of their own charts to play. It wasn't always accepted, however. A band I played with in the northern part of Ohio did a special medley of Christmas hymns only to be stopped while playing it and told such music was sacrilegious! We were told that such music shouldn't be played for dancing!

Arrangers were frequently the difference between a band with a future and one headed downward or forced to fold. The American Federation of Musicians defines arranging as "the art of preparing and adapting an already written composition for presentation in other than its original form… Arranging is the art of giving an existing melody musical variety." The 1930s, '40s and '50s had some talented arrangers handling assignments for major bandleaders who recognized the public's changing tastes. There were lots of unscored collaborative charts called "head arrangements" (in the head of the musician) at the time. Count Basie was famous for head arrangements but the section work of big bands and the need for integrating the harmonies and melodies continued to make arrangements necessary. In fact, a good number of the head arrangements became complete charts in Basie, Woody Herman and Duke Ellington bands and others. Sammy Nestico, Neal Hefti, Don Redman and Billy Strayhorn were early pioneers who were joined by people like Eddie Sauter, Vic Schoen, Pete Rugolo, Oliver Nelson, Johnny Richards, Billy May, Thad Jones, Maria Schneider, Bob Brookmeyer, Steve Sample Sr, Lou Marini, Nelson Riddle, Ralph Burns, Billy Byers, Gordon Jenkins, Ray Conniff, Henry Mancini, Gil Evans, Gordon Goodwin and Ray Reach.

Race restrictions also played a role in limiting the performances of big bands. Bandleaders such as Goodman and Shaw turned down gigs, some lucrative, because proprietors tried to limit the use of black musicians traveling with them.

Whitesboro, NY bandleader and longtime music director, Don Cantwell, remembered that Shaw was told that a black musician had to "sit apart from the band when it played an engagement. Artie said no and that was that."

Women bandleaders and musicians in the big band era were virtually ignored by early music historians until the second half of the 20th century.

The most prominent band of all females was actually led by a man; Phil Spitalny and his Hour of Charm Orchestra. The band, which featured a number of talented women including a trombonist who was the mother of today's famous multi-media and music bandleader, Chip Davis of the Mannheim Steamrollers.

Some have suggested the male leadership of the group was a concession to the view that the business was dominated by men. Ina Ray Hutton toured with her Melodears extensively in the '30s and '40s and drew good crowds, too. Ina, who was chosen by the band's originator, Irving Mills, to front the group didn't really lead the band so much as she offered a floor show as she weaved around the bandstand in a sexy gown. She was promoted as "The Blonde Bombshell of Rhythm."

Most observers believe Spitalny, a Ukrainian born naturalized American, sought a novelty when he organized the all-girl orchestra and soon discovered the popularity of his creation when he went on radio in 1934. His *Hour of Charm* was broadcast on CBS and NBC for 14 years. It was a 22-piece orchestra that was assembled when he joined with Evelyn Kaye Klein to audition more than 1,000 women musicians in New York, Chicago, Cleveland, Detroit and Pittsburgh to find members. He later married Evelyn, who was featured with her "Magic Violin," in 1946.[13]

During the war years (1942-43) a Utica, NY "trumpet boy wonder" who had gained national notoriety on network radio also led an all-female orchestra and went on a countrywide tour playing patriotic songs. B.A.

Rolfe was nearing the end of his career in media and music when he took his female musical group countrywide. He led the *Lucky Strike Dance Hour* orchestra on radio and once hosted his own show called *Rolfe*.

There were others, of course. Anna Mae Winburn and her "own 12 Cotton Club Boys" traveled the country in her truck pulled "RV" playing all kinds of venues.

Glorious Gloria Parker became another woman bandleading star in the 1940s and 50s'. The Brooklyn-born daughter of musician Rita Rose, Gloria studied violin but demonstrated her talent and leadership qualities when she got her own show *The Gloria Parker Show* on WABC coast to coast and entertained audiences playing the marimba, organ and the "glass harp" while leading her Swingphony.

A poster of Anna Mae Winburn and her "own 12 Cotton Club Boys" and her traveling "RV" on a midwest tour.
Photo courtesy James Ronan Collection, IA

It was the largest big band ever led by a female. Gloria performed in soundies and in the early '50s she joined bandleader Vincent Lopez at the Taft Hotel hosting a program called *Shake the Maracas* which gave audience members a chance to compete for prizes playing the maracas with her band.[14]

The territorial musician was as committed to playing quality music and offering his best as well as any advertised touring band. Listen to longtime southern musician and bandleader Henry Mason, who founded Atlanta's *Sentimental Journey Orchestra*, and today leads the *NC Revelers:*

"*Sentimental Journey Orchestra* has been in continuous operation for some 33 years and has played all over the mid-south. Simply put they play the Great American songbook about as well as anyone. After being a part of such an organization for such a long time, it wasn't an easy thing to move away from friends since college days and move to another town. Aside from the band, though, there were few ties left in a town where explosive growth has outstripped all reason and traffic jams happen at 3 a.m. one of those being the last straw."

Its beginning was far from a guarantee of the band's later success. Typical of territorial bands, there was no budget, no place to rehearse and little certainty that the group of musicians could make it. Said Mason when the band was organized "we had a bunch of old stock arrangements and we rehearsed in a mental hospital (some said for good reason) after we were thrown out of a local arts center for making too much noise and disturbing the concentration of the ladies turning pottery wheels." [15]

A bandleader who offers an authentic and entertaining view and sound of the past in the present is Brooks Tegler who heads his own band in Washington, DC.

His band doesn't mimic the greats of long ago, it gives you a feeling and sense of witnessing the reality of Glenn Miller, Tommy Dorsey, Woody Herman, Artie Shaw and others. For example, he lets you understand how bandleaders of the early days gave attention to soloists without stepping away from the dance function of the big band. Says Brooks in an interview with *JazzWax*'s Marc Myers: "Most of the big bands of the 1930s and 1940s had small groups within them. Each band had major players and only in these small groups could players shine. Whether it was the Benny Goodman Quartet, Artie Shaw's Gram-

Brooks Tegler   Photo courtesy of Brooks Tegler

mercy Five, Woody Herman's Woodchoppers or Tommy Dorsey's Clambake Seven, these small groups had a different personality." If you saw and heard those performances as I did you knew how it helped the leader, the players and the audience. Yet it didn't really take away from the evening performance either. It demonstrated the versatility and personality of the musicians. [16]

Not all bandleaders took themselves seriously and discovered the public loved them whether they were absolutely corny or professionally smooth. Ted Lewis, who opened virtually every program with the Depression Era line "Is Everybody Happy?" knew generating fun was powerful in the 1930s. Lewis, who let everyone know he was from Circleville, OH, was recognized as the worst playing clarinetist on the circuit and generally admitted it. Yet, his band was considered an excellent dance band and second in popularity to the King of Jazz Paul Whiteman at the time. He was most astute; he hired the best musicians he could and that included young talent like Benny Goodman, Tommy and Jimmy Dorsey.

Like Lawrence Welk, his band played what people wanted and the public responded with support. His musicians didn't like the popularity of being the corniest band around but they liked the steady work that Lewis gave them.

His band continued into 1960. Lawrence Welk's sidemen complained about the same thing. But they were happy to find the work! And they also were happy that Welk kept a few of them alive. Pete Fountain, legendary New Orleans clarinetist, joined the Welk band later in his career. His comment to Geraldine Wyckoff in a 2001 *Jazz Times* piece tell the story: "Lawrence Welk kept me sober and it damn near killed me. He was pretty hard on drinking."

Years after the Big Band Era evaporated and the ballrooms became derelict buildings, the memories remained vivid for many of us who can still see and hear the music and taste the pretzels and beer.

My memories are still vivid of funny experiences that weren't so humorous at the time. One Saturday night Elks gig was an example. The night was a fun holiday time for players and dancers and the final number came quickly. Packing up a set of drums can be like dismantling a traveling circus. There are packing crates, various sleeves to put together, nuts and bolts to unloosen or take apart and normally you're the last to leave. The piano player is already gone. But on this night, I had a tipsy woman who continued to be fixated on my bass drum. I tried to ignore her but as I lugged the huge Slingerland bass out to the sidewalk so I could make three to four trips for the rest of the equipment she followed. I left the bass on the sidewalk ignoring the fact that I had parked on a steep hill on Main Street. As I walked back inside, I heard a rolling sound and I turned to find she had launched my bass drum on a roll down the hill and it was picking up speed. I dropped everything and raced down the sidewalk still not catching up to the thundering bass. I caught up with it at the bottom of the hill before it would have made it into the intersection and who knows what would have happened! I spent the next week repairing some of the nicks and bruises. Fortunately, I never saw her again.

1. Iowa Public Television "Jack Jenny" www.iptv.org/jazz/Iowa.cfm
2. Lou DiSario, letter, Feb.27, 2002
3. Gary Greenfelder, email, OneBeatBack.com March 13, 2002
4. Eddie Condon's Scrapbook of Jazz, Galahad Books, 1973
5. Chuz Alfred, The Gigography: Reflections on 'The Road' (unpublished) 1994
6. "Swinging to the Tunes of Dick Trimble," Lancaster Eagle-Gazette, July 7, 1993; letter from Paul Kumler, July 27, 2000
7. Letter, Frank Galime, Oct. 21, 2003
8. Sentimental Journey Orchestra, "Bandstand Stories," Henry Mason, www.thesjo.com/page/stories
9. "That Was Then," chapter 7, Stan Kenton: The Early Years 1941-1947, Edward F. Gabel, Balboa Books, 1993
10. E-mail, David Miller, Dec. 24, 2001
11. Partial list of lesser known touring bands, 1930-1965, (appendix) www. Crabapplesound.com/bb-group.htm
12. Scrapbook of Jazz, Eddie Condon
13. en.wikipedia.org/wiki/Phil_Spitalny
14. en.wikipedia.org/wiki/Gloria_Parker
15. Henry Mason, "How It All Happened," Bandstand Stories. www.revorch.com/pages/history/html
16. Jazz Wax: Interview: Marc Myers with Brooks Pegler, April 1, 2009, www.jazzwax.com/2009/04/interview-brooks-tegler.html

Ballrooms

Made the Big Band Era

They were the Hollywood and Vine for millions of young and middle aged during some of the most stressful years of the 20th century.

Ballrooms. Dancing was the popular social activity whether you took Arthur Murray classes or you taught yourself in a corner of the dance floor... with or without a partner! Dancers put a world at war and the struggles from economic and labor strife aside for hours as they glided on the soft wood floor under a kaleidoscope of lights to the music of favorite bands.

There were an estimated 3,000 to 4,000 ballrooms during the Big Band Era and the majority were busy every weekend and some were open nightly during the summers. Preoccupation with television by a later generation replaced them as did the shopping malls of an even later generation who had shed their bobbysox and saddle shoes for flipflops. While ballrooms were disappearing, drive-ins mushroomed. Post-war needs brought road building, new cars and places for families to go which created the demand for fast food establishments. By 1950, there were 1,446 Dairy Queen outlets. Today? It's owned by Berkshire Hathaway and there are more than 6,000 in the United States, Canada and 20 countries throughout the world. The older you get, the more the changes speed past you.

But the ballrooms where the sound erupted on Friday and Saturday nights bring such wonderful memories to so many. Good friend and talented saxophonist Chuz Alfred, offers his feelings about his musical past on the road playing gigs throughout the country: "We remember the ballrooms and the big bands. Loved hearing those sounds! There was an 'air' about the bands. There was an excitement! Remember how it really felt, what was happening? The intensity building as the band 'set up.' Forget the miles they drove just to get there. They will… you will too. Greet a friend, small talk a little… and finally, the time is NOW. The lights come down. The noise fades… and BAM! The air bursts open with sounds. Fast sound. Slow sound. Frantic sound… blue sound. It was fantastic! Then before you knew it, the air suddenly fused back together and the sounds were gone. Done. Finished. The night was expended. Musicians had come together for a moment. They were the happening. And now, they're gone… on the road to somewhere else. Another place in time where they'll magically appear and another 'happening' will begin. Sometimes, we knew where and when it was going to be. Make your plans…GO!"

Said the National Ballroom & Entertainment Association (NBEA) about the evolution: "Although ballrooms have long been associated with the big bands, it was the Jazz Age where many of them got their start. The '30s and '40s were undoubtedly the highpoint of the ballroom era and, ironically, it was the end of War World II that also saw the downsizing in the number of ballrooms across the United States. Many ballrooms remained quite prominent through the '30s and into the '60s. But by the later '60s, changing times began to take a heavy toll on those popular dance locales. Ballrooms could be elegant or plain. They could be in the biggest cities or in the smallest rural areas of the country. But they shared a common denominator of music and dancing. For many decades the ballroom was the dominate place for social gatherings."

An essay in the *St. James Encyclopedia of Pop Culture (Jan. 29, 2002)* by Ethan Hay explained the power of dancing and ballrooms in America. Said Hay: "Many famous dance venues from the Cotton Club and Roseland in New York, the Avalon Ballroom on Catalina Island, Aly Baba in Oakland, to the Old Roosevelt Hotel in New Orleans, attest to the tremendous influence which dancing has had on American Culture… Local community dance halls thrive in recreation centers, churches and high school gymnasia as well as commercial night clubs… An important concept of the dance hall is 'to see and be seen' and rites of passage into society including coming-of-age events, proms and pageants, ceremonies such as weddings, and musical debuts have centered around dance events and subsequently are popular uses for dance halls." Hay explains that it was the polka that ignited dancing and the need for dance halls in the United States as wave upon wave of immigrants from Poland, forced to leave by the Nazis, streamed to America.

Dancing languished when the 1950s became the l960s and 1970s and young people found other interests, other pastimes. Ballrooms, social clubs and even hotels continued to close reducing convenient dancing sites. But things began to change as the 20th century became the 21st. Said Gary Strauss of *USA TODAY:* "Ballroom dancing, as a media phenomenon, sport, hobby and business, is enjoying its biggest resurgence since the 1940s. Arthur Murray, No.1 in the $500 million lessons market, says business among 155 US franchisees is up sharply…"

The last of the ballrooms in the Detroit area were the Edgewater Park which burned down in 1954, Jefferson Beach's Pavilion which became a boathouse in 1955, the Graystone which sold in 1957 and the Vanity which ended in 1959.

The Walled Lake Casino struggled but remained open until its last night in September, 1960.

Looking back, some ballrooms have history that parallels their communities. In Boston, **Moseley's On The Charles** (www.moseleyson-thecharles) has remained a landmark for over 100 years and today is believed to be the oldest continuous running ballroom in the country.

It began as a summer canoe house and a ballroom on the banks of the Charles River in Dedham, MA, by Elisha Moseley in 1905. All the touring bands did one niters at Moseley's sometime during their tenure. Guy Lombardo, Harry James, Les Brown, Buddy Rich, Lester Lanin were frequent visitors and so were rockers like The Platters, the Marvelettes, the Grass Roots, the Manhattans and comedians such as Pat Cooper. In 1998, local resident Edward DeVincenzo, a former employee who began his years of work in the coatroom, bought the establishment and renovated it to give this picturesque ballroom a future.

Most eastern dancers who loved fast, sensual, scat dancing remember the **Savoy Ballroom** which, for 32 years (1926 to 1958) made popular what was called the "Home of Happy Feet." It was one of the first integrated ballrooms and gave fans and bands roots for big band music and innovative and dynamic dancing. The Lindy Hop dance step started there and regulars knew that the best of the best at the ballroom congregated every evening in the northeast corner in a place called "Cat's Corner."

Unlike many ballrooms you walked into from the street, the Savoy (www.wikipedia.org/wiki/Savoy_Ballroom) was on the second floor of a block long building where it welcomed black and white dancers during years when segregation was an issue. It didn't hesitate to take on the race conflict, either. The Savoy frequently staged "Battle of the Bands" promotions that put the house band, usually black bandleader Chick Webb and his group, against others like white bandleader Benny Goodman, and let the crowd determine the winner. Webb's band usually won, newspapers reported. Goodman and Count Basie were both losers to the popular Webb band. Dancers called the ballroom "The Track" because of the elongated shape of the floor. The establishment, which could accommodate up to 5,000, was located in Harlem at Lenox Avenue between 140th and 141st Streets.

Pink on the inside with its' mirrored walls, the Savoy had a double bandstand, a larger one and a medium sized band shell along its east wall and had over a 10,000 square feet of spring loaded wooden dance floor to ease dancing pleasure. More than 250 bands, national touring groups and territorial, were featured at the Savoy over its lifetime. Bands worked in tandem and music was continuous as one band was always in a position to pick up the beat and melody of a number. Bands traded arrangements at the transition from one band to another. Dancing usually wasn't possible when the battles were waged because of the crowded conditions. The very popular 1934 big band classic song *"Stompin' at the Savoy"* recorded by many touring groups debuted at the Savoy.

Management served soft drinks, wine or beer and offered ice cream drinks and dishes including banana splits, sundaes and floats, a popular menu for many dancing establishments in the 1930s, '40s and '50s.

The West Coast had its featured spots like Cotillion Hall (today the **Crystal Ballroom**) at 1332 West Burnside in Portland, OR. The 95-year-old ballroom was first owned by Montrose Ringler but financial difficulties forced a sale to Dad Watson in the 1920s when it sponsored more square dances than big band dancing. It was purchased again in the 1930s and changed its name to the Crystal. In the 1960s, the ballroom featured such acts as James Brown, Marvin Gaye and Ike & Tina Turner, the Grateful Dead and others and became the residence for squatters and art types. The ballroom ownership became concerned about the music and the psychedelic acts of the late 1960s and it stopped such performances. In 1979, the building was listed on the National Register of Historic Places.

Back East, dancers and those interested in weekend fun showed up by the thousands at Atlantic City's **Steel Pier Marine Ballroom** where you could find the top big bands during any summer. One hundred eleven years later, still standing and still attracting crowds long after the big band era disappeared, the Steel Pier has that history so rich with personal stories. In the 1950s and '60s, a Fourth of July weekend would feature a Ray Charles Show on Sunday-Monday, the Dave Clark Five on the Fourth and finish a day later with Paul Revere & The Raiders.

From 1920 through the final days of the touring bands, everyone in the band business had played the Steel Pier at least once and many were back a number of times. It was Amusement City, right across from the Taj Mahal Resort and Casino, and it became the "Showplace of the Nation" to those who enjoyed it. Miss America was crowned there for four years and you could count on a crowd of 80,000 on the Sunday before Labor Day annually.

During the '40s and '50s, Guy Lombardo and his Royal Canadians were there along with Benny Goodman, Jimmy Dorsey, Frank Sinatra, Gene Krupa, the Dukes of Dixieland, Harry

Steel Pier program

Photo courtesy of Lou DiSario

James, Bob Crosby and his BobCats, Lee Castle, Jimmy Palmer, Clyde Mc-Coy, Buddy Rich and Art Mooney and his *I'm Looking Over a Four-Leaf Clover* band and Louie Armstrong came a few times.

Jim Ellis in his web site www.steel-pier.com probably summed up the Atlantic City spot the best: "I'm not knocking gambling at all. I just have the opinion that Atlantic City has a very proud past and that past should not be limited to a museum. I would love to see a new, old Steel Pier. I would love it to be built with the original blueprints. I think it's a sad mistake not having several amusement piers there."

Less than a few hundred miles away, a hotel ballroom gained as much notoriety for a telephone number as it did for its accommodations. **The Hotel Pennsylvania**, home at one time of legendary Glenn Miller and his civilian band and the site of a famous telephone number Pennyslvania 6-5000 (the real number was 736-5000 but Glenn made it Pennsylvania 6-5000).

The action took place at the hotel's **Café Rouge**, a red-walled room with red drapes and a capacity of 600, which was filled nightly as people came to hear Glenn, Count Basie, Duke Ellington, Benny Goodman, Harry James, the Dorsey Brothers, Artie Shaw and hundreds of other touring big bands. In 1940, you could get a single room for $3.50. When it was built it was the world's largest hotel with 2,200 rooms and high rise elevators. And if you couldn't get there you always had radio remotes coast to coast to hear the band of the evening. Close your eyes and envision the Miller band at the Café and scan the bandstand. You can see young men like trumpeters Billy May and Ray Anthony, bassist Rollie Bundock, tenor saxophonist Tex Beneke, clarinet Willie Schwartz, drummer Mo Purtell playing fresh new music or the favorites *In the Mood, Moonlight Serenade* and the brand new *Pennsylvania 6-5000.* Just months before the band arrived for its engagement at the Café it had turned the corner financially with big nights at **Paradise Restaurant**, Frank Dailey's **Meadowbrook** and the **Glen Island Casino**.

Jimmy Dorsey
Photo courtesy of the James Ronan Collection, IA

May, who wrote for Miller, told how bandsmen remembered the Hotel and Café Rouge: "There was a bar across from the bandstand at the Café Rouge. 'Kelly's Bar' I think but anyway you could see straight across the street to where we played. Frankie D'Annolfo was the timekeeper when we took a break and when the bartender at Kelly's or whatever the bar was called would see him back on the stand he'd say 'Time for one more fellas… Frankie's on the bandstand.'"

A ballroom in the midwest that took your breath away because of its size and ambiance was **The Aragon** in Chicago, five miles north of downtown in a neighborhood known as "Uptown." It was built in 1926 by brothers William and Andrew Karzas at an astounding cost for the time; nearly two million dollars. It was an ideal location; near the well-known "L," Chicago's elevated railway. Considering admission price of admission (50 cents) the ballroom on Winthrop and Lawrence Avenues became a showplace not merely in the Windy City but the midwest.

The brothers Karzas actually built two "wonder ballrooms" *Time Magazine* said in a New Year's Eve story, 1946. They built the **Trianon** on the south side of the city and **Aragon** on the north. The ballrooms averaged $4,000 a week and frequently created new bands to create even more excitement.

The **Aragon** dance floor covered more than 80,000 square feet and could feature two bands without causing difficulty for the audience. It was in a class of its own said many who visited it. Unfortunately, it had lost some of that luster when I visited it in the late 1960s but you could see remnants of its ornate beauty and if you closed your eyes you could hear the big band sounds.

It was designed to replicate a Spanish palace courtyard with its crystal chandeliers, mosaic tiles, garishly painted plaster, terra-cotta ceiling and beautiful arches and featured a huge dance floor that rested on a cushion of cork, felt and springs. Men were obligated to wear jackets and ties and women wore semi-formal evening wear. There was no smoking on the second floor and tuxedoed floor walkers made sure that close dancing and jitterbugging was kept in check. But the rules didn't bother the crowds; weekly attendance topped 18,000 during the 1920s, 30s and 40s. It was called the most beautiful dance hall in America. Bill Karzas never took the time to polish his language which was pidgeon Greek from his native country but his meaning was quite clear when he told an interviewer: "We think what people want, we appeal to the five senses. We give good music for ear, beautiful place for eye, fresh air for smell, good chairs for comfort, and special ice cream for taste."

But he had old fashioned morals too. He made sure the ballroom hosted a singles night for those who were lonely and a "Married Couples" night for those celebrating their vows. He was proud of the fact that one such night brought 800 couples to the ballroom. And while he only charged a $1.25 a person, he grossed over a million each year.

Every name big band and a number of territorial groups played the **Aragon** offering it the status of separating orchestras that had "arrived" from others. Julia Galas has vivid memories of the ballroom. "The year was 1941, and the man packing 'em into the **Aragon Ballroom** was Glenn Miller. Usually there was no room to dance; we just stood there listening to the good music. There was one band that had even more people than Glenn Miller and that was Kay Kyser… Years later, I remember seeing Dick Jurgens in another crowded place and he said, 'My gosh, this looks like my old Aragon crowd." Furthermore, it could be considered the "Vegas" of the midwest. Many singles became couples at the ballroom and later married.

Said Manager Liz Varney: "This place in the '50s and '60s was really popular for ballroom dancing. It was a big turning point for a lot of groups. If you can fill a place with 4,500 people the next step is pretty big."

Another Chicago dancing hall is also remembered by locals and others in the region.

Called **Byrd Ballroom**, it was located on West Madison near Cicero

Avenue in the city. Actually, it was on the second floor of the Byrd Theatre, a movie house.

It was named after a hero of the period, Admiral Byrd, who discovered both the North and South Poles, but most don't believe he ever danced in the building.

Chicagoan Phil Holdman, president of the *Browsers*, remembered it fondly in an April, 2005 edition of his publication. "The room served sandwiches and drinks on the mezzanine. A great Italian beef sandwich was only 25 cents. A stein of Pabst Blue Ribbon was also a quarter. So, during intermission, the boys would go to the tavern next door and get a stein of beer for a dime…" The dance floor was always sparkling clean and the dancers loved it. The patrons usually dressed formal on Saturday nights. Bandleader Carl Schreiber played an alto sax or, once in a while, played a chorus on his Celeste. Carl didn't tolerate swearing either—the worst he ever said when he got angry was 'For cry bones!"

The **Arcadia**, one of uptown Chicago's most popular spots, gave those in the Windy City a number of ballrooms to visit. While many city ballroom managers were rigid on race issues, promoter Paddy Harmon, who owned other entertainment spots, had no problem hiring all-black bands. The reason, many said, was that black bands were less orchestrated and that appealed to younger crowds. In the mid-1920s, bands like Walter Barnes and his Royal Creolians and Charles Elgar and his Orchestra were at the **Arcadia**. Barnes was well known later for the shows he did for Al Capone and his Cicero **Cotton Club**.

But the midwest had many ballrooms, family-owned, and places that became community gathering places. John Matter, who was an influential voice for years in Iowa ballrooms and whose family owned and operated the **Matter Ballroom** in Decorah, IA, said ballrooms offered the ambiance that other structures didn't have. "A ballroom was designed to hold large crowds. There is just

In the ballroom, you were a participant, not a spectator.

something about a large crowd sharing an exciting experience. As a ballroom operator these magical moments can give you a chill. It's not the same as a concert or some other experiences. In the ballroom, you were a participant, not a spectator." It was simple as that.

Ballrooms, of course, could come in all shapes and locations. The

Roseland Ballroom, which began originally in Philadelphia in 1917 was torn down and moved to West 52nd Street, New York City in 1956. But in the 1920s while money flowed on Wall Street and elsewhere people were excited about the new dance crazes and the Roseland became a focal point. Fletcher Henderson was Manhattan's top band and his music catered to those who could turkey trot as well as foxtrot. The 'Charleston' was just making its appearance and Fletcher's saxophonist Don Redman was arranging music that featured new improvisations for an 11 piece band. Paul Whiteman may have been crowned "King of Jazz" but in Manhattan and other parts of New York City Fletcher was considered the legitimate "King of Jazz. "Redman introduced brass sections and reeds playing against one other adding something new to contemporary swing music.

Time Magazine described Roseland's interior as "purple-and-cerise tentlike décor that creates a definite harem effect." Its New York owner, Louis Brecker, converted it to a roller skating rink first and then turned it into a dance hall which promoted ballroom dancing but banned rock and roll as well as disco. Brecker told reporters in the 1970s that his establishment wanted to bring back "cheek-to-cheek dancing, it's what this place is all about." When it began it could accommodate 3,500 or a dance party of 2,500. Its racial policy at the outset was a "whites only" dance club and it claimed to be the home of "refined dancing."

That changed over the years and Count Basie was partially responsible for bringing the change to the "whites only" edict. The Count introduced a popular swing number *The Roseland Shuffle* while playing the Roseland.

A dance spot that some contend launched the "swing" era was the **Palomar Ballroom** in Los Angeles, CA which owed much to Benny Goodman on his first trip to the west coast. Benny arrived at the ballroom in the middle of the Depression in his own depression over the lack of crowds along his trip.

At the time, it was considered the largest and most famous dance halls on the west coast. It could accommodate 4,000 couples which had to excite Benny and frighten him at the same time. His music simply wasn't drawing crowds until, according to press reports, his second set when he tossed his book and inserted Fletcher Henderson's arrangements and the band and an influx of hundreds of more fans gave him a rousing return to the east. It was Aug. 21, 1935, and two years later the Palomar box office sales broke 50,000 and Benny became "king of swing." The ballroom featured everything to make it an amusement park under roof; an indoor miniature golf course, klieg lights illuminating a minaret structure on the roof and a 7,500 square foot patio which created its first title, "El Patio Ballroom." It drew large crowds by nightly radio broadcasts from KFLJ which told listeners the ballroom was the "Dancing, Dining and Entertainment Center of the West." It was destroyed by fire in the winter, 1939, while Charley Barnet was playing the site. It cost Charley his instruments, all his arrangements and other paraphernalia. Billy May, then doing freelance work for bands, spent hours re-arranging Charley's charts so he could continue.

Spanish themes were popular during the 1920s it seems. The **Indiana Ballroom**, which opened Sept. 7, 1927, with Marion McKay's *Kings of Tempo*, looked like the courtyard of a Spanish coastal village complete with night sky that offered twinkling stars, clouds and that romantic crescent moon. You got all that for an admission price of $1 for men and 75 cents for women which included checking coats and hats. But the management asked patrons to refrain from tipping! The touring bands put Indiana on their schedule as they came from the Aragon or headed southeast for Sandusky, OH's **Cedar Point Ballroom**. Just a few miles beyond, dancers could meet at Geneva-on-the-Lake to hear the sounds and stretch their legs to most of the touring bands at the **Pier Dance Hall**. The '40s saw Geneva build a mile long entertainment "strip" of businesses. Young people from the tri-state region came to hear the big bands, try the beaches and enjoy themselves. Bandleader Kay Kyser never forgot it. Kay, locals said, was marooned and broke when he and his musicians disbanded at the ballroom. According to the stories, he spent the rest of the summer living off the generosity of the Bowers, proprietors of the Shady Beach Hotel, as he put his career back together. And quite a career it was on radio, television and in the movies. Meanwhile, ballrooms in nearby Cleveland were trying to relax the strict dancing regulations the city council adopted for area ballrooms in the mid-1920s. Here's a sample from Section 8 of Ordinance No. 20456-A: "Vulgar, noisy jazz music is prohibited. Such music almost forces dancers to use jerky half-steps and invites immoral variations."

Peter Levinson, author of a good biography of Tommy Dorsey called *Tommy Dorsey: Livin' in a Great Big Way* describes how dancing was a part of growing up in eastern Pennsylvania where the Dorsey brothers began in the band business. Fire destroyed a major ballroom in the Scranton, PA area but the **Lakeside Ballroom** was restored and continues today. The ethnics—Irish, Welsh, Poles, and Italians— in the region were dancers and consequently, the Dorsey Brothers found plenty of opportunities for their talents. The ballrooms were less than half a mile apart and while they were competitive, dances were held at both on Thursday and Saturday nights. "It is a quite remarkable statement about how much dancing meant to that area that they could, for decades, have two dance halls host large music events on a twice a week basis," Levinson wrote. Few disagree with the assessment.

Folks in Schuyler, NE have nostalgic memories of **The Oak Ballroom** and it only demonstrates how important such buildings were to the community. The ballroom fed the area's culture and entertainment and, at the same time, put food on local families' tables, too. Unemployment in the mid-1930s had reached 33 percent and the gloom was as heavy as the fog of late summer and early autumn nights. But a major recovery act called the WPA brought work and in 1937 the completion of **The Oak Ballroom**, a community asset that citizens look to with pride revitalized the region… and certainly put weekly dances on social calendars.

In southern Ohio more ballrooms attracted dancers of all ages. At Buckeye Lake, OH, a manmade body of water, crowds came every summer by cars and buses.

Listen to Maurice Ludwig, a Buckeye Lake native who returned after WWII to work for A.M. Brown, the park manager: "Like the song goes (1949) it 'was a good year.' We had Ray Anthony in and a couple of so-called country music bands which turned out to be more hillbilly music

The Crystal Ballroom   Photo courtesy of the Buckeye Lake (OH) Museum

but the rest of the park did pretty well. Everybody made a few dollars and things looked pretty good. The year after the war ended, Stan Billows was the ballroom manager and I helped him out with his broadcasting every evening and I had to fill in introducing the bands. I remember we had Chick Webb, Anthony and Leo Reichert and others. Anthony was the house band at the **Crystal Ballroom**, the Ink Spots were in and Bunny Berigan served as a house band for a week or so. He died not long after he played the lake. Gus Arnheim was another band and we got Fletcher Henderson, who was very well liked but Brownie wouldn't book him because he had played the Lake Breeze Hotel and that was that! Brownie wouldn't book you if you played for a lake competitor. One of the things that I'll never forget was the big bell we had with a large clapper and long lanyard. The 1st night Glenn Miller was there he played '*Pennsylvania 6-5000*' and one of the sidemen found the lanyard to the bell so when they reached the phrase '6500' he pulled it and you could hear the bell all over the park. He almost broke the cord he pulled it so hard. The band and the audience laughed and screamed and needless to say they played that song more than once

that night." LUD remembers the money flowed from appearances of big bands. "When Glenn Miller played the lake he was on the way up and on the road and really hot! Brownie booked him the first time for something like $1,000 on short notice. We had about 3,000 that night. We booked him two years later and the cost was $6,000. The first time our admission price was a $1. The second time he appeared we charged $2.50 a head and we had between 9,000 and 9,500 people."

Bunny Berigan Photo courtesy of the James Ronan Collection, IA

Billow was the creative thrust behind many of Buckeye Lake park signs that covered the lakefront amusement center each summer. He also played a large role in a publication called *The Resorter*. He held dual roles for a period as park publicity director and **Crystal Ballroom** manager. To many I talked to, Stan was a steady, tireless park activist who promoted 24/7 and "who never seemed to get much mention even though he was felt to have brought greatness to a spot that possibly wouldn't have survived without such effort," one said. Like others in the tightly knit circle of big band aficionados who managed and promoted ballrooms from Atlantic City to Miami, Chicago and Los Angeles, Stan's friends were in high places in the band business; Glenn Miller, Tommy and Jimmy Dorsey, Stan Kenton among others. At Stan's death, the outpouring of condolences came from bandleaders throughout the country.

Balmy evenings, a midway crammed with people and music drifting from the open air pavilions like the **Pier Ballroom** at one end of the Buckeye Lake Park and the **Crystal** at the other were what motivated LUD. "One evening we had Stan Kenton booked and one of my helpers came running up to tell me that a lady singer needed a place to change clothes, "he told me. "That's how I met June Christie. She was standing not far away from a line of women waiting to use the lone ladies room. I took her back to the skate room (in the roller rink) which was the only room with a lock that I knew about. She said that would be fine and asked me to stand guard and not let anyone in… not even Stan, she said with a smile. She came out about 10 minutes later and gave me a gentle hug and a big smile and headed for the bandstand. Needless to say, I've got every one of her recordings."

You never knew what to expect when dealing with celebrities on the road doing one nighters. Every event could be a new experience, he said. "Paul Whiteman played the skating rink and his two buses showed up just ahead of show time," he remembered. "There was a scramble to get last minute details taken care of, instruments offloaded, music in place and all that and I noted that Whiteman was nonchalant about it all. He was a very distinguished looking gentleman even when he wasn't dressed to perform. He had a great band of excellent musicians. Minutes later, he gave the downbeat for his theme and the dancing began. Then, it seems, he disappeared. He was gone most of the rest of the night in fact. A band member suggested we might find him in one of the buses. Sure enough, he was sound asleep with an alcohol aroma that took your breath away which explained his absence."

Not far away, east of Buckeye Lake was **Lake Park Pavilion** of Coshocton, OH, located in a county with a cluster of lakes. The Pavilion was the creative project of Dick and Helen Johns who spent years in vaudeville and theater ownership and moved to Coshocton in 1922 and realized their dream. Dick built the Pavilion the next year and worked to bring the dance bands to a rural part of Ohio. Said Fred Workman, a Coshocton historian and a former lifeguard at the park: "Dick… had many name bands such as Sammy Kaye and Les Brown playing here for special dances. We always had a lot of kids and grown-ups here for those dances. There were a lot of memories here. Not only of swimming and dancing but other activities that were put on here. A lot of people came here to walk on the board walk and listen to the bands." Similar to the **Pier** and **Crystal Ballrooms** at Buckeye Lake and other summer ballrooms around the country, the **Lake Park Pavilion** had wooden windows that were opened when weather permitted so the music wafted outside.

Lakes, of course, were an attraction to dancers and musicians alike. Maurice Ludwig told of bandleaders and sidemen getting special privileges to swim in nearby pools after hours. In Central New York, Russell's Danceland at Sylvan Beach, NY, a large barn like building was an exciting dance hall for thousands of New Yorkers on the shores of Oneida Lake. During the 1940s, a summer schedule would feature one nighters by bands like Louis Armstrong, Sammy Kaye, Duke Ellington, Cab Calloway, Gene Krupa, Lionel Hampton and more than 100 others. Former radio announcer and big band aficionado Bob Montesano Sr of Utica, NY, had fond memories of his radio remotes at various dances. "My fondness for big band music really grew listening to late night music from big hotels around the country. I felt like I was there. We did local remotes from an outside dance setting at Bennett's Field near Utica. The bands I recall most from my announcing days were Chuck Foster, Bob Chester and singer Bob Eberle who also had a band at the time. My favorite was Foster because he was friendly and did not appear to throw his 'importance' around like other celebrities I met in those days…"

Communities with connections to movies and stars could generate plenty of excitement for big bands too. That plus World War II virtually assured **The Hollywood Palladium** a gigantic leap forward when it opened Sept. 23, 1940, on the site of the old Paramount Pictures. It created a spectacular event that other ballroom owners envied.

Popular Tommy Dorsey and his band featuring Buddy Rich and singer Connie Haines and a frail vocalist with a powerful voice, Frank Sinatra, brought swooning women by cars, trains and buses. Opening night at the Palladium had an SRO crowd of more than 6,500 at each show on its 11,200 foot dance floor. What better address for a ballroom than Sunset Boulevard. Connie remembered the opening night for years. It was her 21st birthday and no one during the day said anything about it. She and Jackie Cooper were planning to spend an evening together but Tommy told the band and singers not to leave because they needed to rehearse new numbers right after the last show. Lonely and unhappy, she went back to the Palladium stage to rehearse and Tommy struck up the band with "Happy Birthday Connie" and she was a part of a surprise party, cake, close friends and all. Later she said: "It was the kind of day and night one doesn't easily forget. It was special."

During WWII, soldiers, sailors and airmen stationed around California loved going to meet movie and music stars at the Hollywood Canteen and visit the Palladium just down the street. Virtually every touring name band appeared at the Palladium during the war and its radio remotes let the country share the music and the programs.

But ironically it wasn't the war years that welcomed the largest crowd. Says the Palladium web site: "Even after the war, when big bands began to lose their popularity, the Palladium still drew in a record 6,750 eager dancers to the January, 1947 opening night performance of Tex Beneke and the Glenn Miller Orchestra—an event enthusiastically covered by *Life Magazine*."

The reorganization of the Miller band post-war with remnants of the military band was a shrewd business move although it was also a calculated risk. The band business was slipping rapidly as ballrooms closed. It was a different Miller band stateside fans heard at the Palladium that night. Like Harry James, the other major name band on the road, Tex added 13 violinists and traveled with 31 sidemen, a far cry from the 1938 band that featured 15 to 16 musicians.

Leo McElroy remembers his own Palladium years as an announcer for KFI radio when he worked a regional network doing "Saturday Night Dance Party."

"It was mid to late 1960s," he recalled, "I got assigned to do the 9 p.m. live half-hour pick-up of Lawrence Welk from the Palladium. Then, while colleague Dick Sinclair did the 10 p.m. pick-up of Freddy Martin from the Coconut Grove at the Ambassador Hotel, I drove like hell to Glendora on the outskirts to do the 11 p.m. pick-up of Johnny Catron's big band from Glendora Palms… which was far and away the best live music of the night."

The Welk show was a no-brainer, he said. "I would introduce the maestro, get off the stage, grab a bite to eat (free!) and I was back on stage in time to sign off. The musicians I talked to griped a lot about Welk's shlocky arrangements but it was steady work and they accepted the paychecks. At the Glendora Palms, though, it was much more fun. I introduced the numbers and I was up with the band throughout the evening. I got my training doing live pick-ups on CBS New Year's Eve parties in 1961-1962 with Freddy Martin and Russ Morgan."

Welk, of course, gave the Palladium tremendous notoriety in 1961 when he signed a lifetime contract to syndicate his "Champagne Music" from the Palladium on network TV. He was magnetic to the public and proprietors.

Ballrooms had an atmosphere and ambiance all their own to many who grew up with them. Ginnie of North Carolina, a transplanted native of Wellesley Hills, MA, described her feelings about Norumbega Park, an entertainment site with a penny arcade, huge Ferris wheel, a zoo and most important, a dance pavilion named the **Totem Pole Ballroom** in a blog called goldendaze-ginnie.blogspot.com. The Totem Pole was special to her.

"Virtually every famous swing band appeared there… Benny Goodman, Artie Shaw, Harry James, the Dorsey Brothers… everyone. And the music was broadcast nationally on NBC, ABC and CBS networks," she recalls nostalgically.

"As I remember they didn't have a name band the night that we were there but that didn't dim our enthusiasm. I was mesmerized the minute we walked in. We were on the upper level of a huge hall. A large staircase led down to the main dance floor and couches and small tables were interspersed on the way down. There were actually three dance floors. The enormous one in front of the live orchestra and two smaller ones on either side with seating arrangements. It was all very posh and incredibly romantic. The lighting was soft and the music was dreamy and just right for slow dancing. I doubt if I was as much enthralled by my date as I was the idea of it all; but, it was certainly a night to remember. During the night, I couldn't help but wondering if it was occupied by Totem Pole ghosts of the past… romantic couples on our dance floor, swaying to the hypnotic swing tunes that dominated the '50s and '60s." The Totem Pole is gone… came to an end in 1964. Today a Marriott Hotel is there but the memories linger forever."

Tommy Dorsey

Today? There are approximately 80 ballrooms left in the United States, according to the National Ballroom & Entertainment Association which tracks ballroom activities.

Maintaining the structures and trying to promote the values in another era are quite difficult. Too often, they are simply too financially risky for investors. For example before the 2010 season opened, a $635 million takeover of the Cedar Point, OH amusement park by a global management company was ended when it found weak support from potential investors. The Cedar Point facility included a famous ballroom that entertained many name bands from the 1930s through the 1950s.

"Ballrooms, like other businesses have needed to evolve in order to survive," John Matter of NBEA says. "What kept the doors open 20 years ago is not going to going to pay the bills today. Those ballrooms that have survived deserve a pat on the back. But the future is not bright. Competition for the entertainment dollar is fierce and often times unfair to the ballroom operation. Legislative, licensing and insurance issues have all but closed many ballrooms. The bands will outlive the ballrooms, the venues will be different and the bands will be fewer and smaller in the years to come."

Yet, historic ballrooms continue in our midst, kept alive by country clubs, fraternal associations and lodges and other umbrella associations. They are less likely to be open for dancing but they are used for community social events. For example, on the outskirts of New Hartford, NY a well respected golf club, the **Yahnundasis**, continues operation and holds an occasional dance usually at the holidays. Its history was made in the spring of 1939 when New Hartford High School students decided to hire a Harlem dance band for its spring prom. The band? Drummer Chick Webb… and with him that night was a 22-year-old singer who was attracting praise for her vocals. Ella Fitzgerald made her upstate New York debut for a group of high school dancers. While neither Ella nor Chick were college graduates, it was a Yale University gig where she became a regular with the Harlem Savoy Ballroom-based group. Four years later, fresh from her 1938 New York City hit *A-Tisket, A-Tasket* which she co-wrote, she was one of two singers with the band.

Former ballroom owner and president of the NBEA John Matter remembers the struggle to keep his ballroom operating from the 1970s to the 1990s. "When it came to big band or oldtime dances, they were something I did with the hopes of at least breaking even. And it was great if you could actually make some money on these dances. But I did them because it was something I felt almost a moral obligation to do. The people that still come to these dances were the ones that made your business successful years ago. You feel like this is a way to repay them. However, the ownership of ballrooms today is changing to another generation. I don't believe they feel that link to the past and will continue the music only if it is profitable. Financially, that is not reasonable just unfortunate."

While major ballrooms got occasional national attention, the thousands of community ballrooms that served as social gathering centers bring memories, even tears, from dance band fans I talked to and who wrote me after my book *Big Bands & Great Ballrooms* (AuthorHouse/2006) was published. My research along with my collaboration with the National Ballroom & Entertainers Association (NBEA) found the following ballrooms important to various regions of the country but are merely representatives of the larger number of ballrooms and dancing spots in the early days of the big band era:

Eastern Ballrooms

St. Regis Hotel, NYC; Metropole, NYC; Arthur's, NYC; Rainbow Grill, NYC; Riverboat, NYC; Village Gate, NYC; Waldorf Astoria, NYC; Hotel Taft, NYC; Blue Room, Hotel Lincoln, NYC; Roosevelt Hotel, NYC; Hotel New Yorker, NYC; Biltmore Hotel, NYC; New Zanzibar, NYC; Hotel Astor, NYC; Yacht Club, NYC; Hotel Piccadilly, NYC; Hotel Edison, NYC; Americana Hotel, NYC; Birdland, NYC; Hotel McAlpin, NYC; Avalon, NYC; Steel Pier, Atlantic City, NJ; Terrace Room, Newark, NJ; Hotel Syracuse, Syracuse, NY; Commodore Hotel, NYC; Bill Green's, Pittsburgh, PA; Queensbury Hotel, Glens Falls, NY; The Plaza, Manhattan, NY; The Carlyle Hotel, NYC; Trinkaus Manor, Oriskany, NY; Hotel Utica, Utica, NY; Russell's Danceland, Sylvan Beach, NY; Franklin Plaza Ballroom, Troy, NY; The Totem Pole, Auburndale, MA; Ritz Ballroom, Pleasure Beach Amusement Park, Bridgeport, CT; Butterfly Ballroom, Springfield, MA; Raynor Ballroom, Roseland State Ballroom, The Wonderland, Spanish Gables Ballroom, Boston; Kimball's Starlight, Lynnfield, MA; The Arcadia, Manchester, NH; Sunset Ballroom, Almonesson, NJ; Meadowbrook, Cedar Grove, NJ; Glen Island Casino, New Rochelle, NY; Oaklyn Dance Ballroom , Oaklyn, NJ; Garden Pier Ballroom, Ocean City, NJ; Ivystone Ballroom, Pennsauken, NJ; Starlite, Ballroom, Wildwood, NJ; Dellwood Ballroom, Crystal Ballroom, Buffalo, NY; George F. Johnson Pavilion, Johnson City, NY; Stardust Ballroom, Savoy Ballroom, NYC; Fiesta Danceteria, Cinderella Ballroom, NYC; Greystone Ballroom, Utica, NY; Castle Rock Ballroom, Allentown, PA; Sunset Pavilion, Carrolltown, PA; Starlight Ballroom, Hershey, PA; Danceland, Westview Park, PA; Lakewood Pavilion, Mahoney City, PA; Brookline on the Boulevard, Wagner Hall Ballroom, Oakes Ballroom, Trianon Ballroom, Elite Ballroom, The Met Ballroom, Garden Ballroom, Raburn Plaza, Philadelphia, PA; Aragon, Savoy, Cottage Inn, The Jitterbug, Savoy Grotto, Garden Plantation, Syrian Mosque, Pittburgh, PA; Sommerton Springs Ballroom, Sommerton, PA; Covered Wagon Ballroom, Upper Darby, PA; Willowgrove Park Ballroom, Willowgrove, PA; Valencia Ballroom, York; Bach Dance Auditorium, Lancaster, PA; Arcadia Ballroom, Providence, RI; Famous, Alcazar Ballrooms, Baltimore, MD; Grossinger's Catskill Hotel, Catskill, NY; Rhodes on the Pawtuxet Ballroom, RI; Nuttings on the Charles, Waltham, MA;

Midwest Ballrooms

London House, Chicago, IL; Safari Hotel, Chicago; Palmer House, Chicago, IL; Drake Hotel, Chicago, IL; LaSalle Hotel, Chicago, IL; Hotel Bismarck, Chicago, IL; Congress Hotel, Chicago, IL; Sign of the Drum, Cincinnati, OH; Blackhawk Restaurant, Chicago, IL; Melody Mill, Chicago, IL; Chez Peree, Chicago, IL; Cedar Point Ballroom, Sandusky, OH; Edgewater Beach Hotel, Chicago, IL; Willbrook Ballroom, Chicago, IL; The Byrd Ballroom, Chicago, IL; Statler Hotel, Cleveland, OH; Milford Ballroom, Chicago, IL; Hotel Sherman, Chicago, IL; Hub Ballroom, Peoria, IL; Hotel St. Paul, St. Paul, MN; Valley Dale Ballroom, Columbus, OH; Pier & Crystal Ballrooms, Buckeye Lake, OH; Casa Loma Ballroom, St. Louis, MO; Cobblestone Ballroom, Storm Lake, IA; The Pier Dance Hall, Geneva-On-The-Lake, OH; The Glen Club, Glenview, Glenview, IL; Luna Pier Ballroom, Erie, MI; Starlite Ballroom, Cincinnati, OH; Yankee Lake Ballroom, Brookfield, OH; Avon Oaks Ballroom, Girard, OH; Melody Lane Ballroom, Newton Falls, OH; Antler's Grand Ballroom, Lorain, OH; Sammy's Marakiki Ballroom, Willoughby, OH; American Ballroom Center, Medina, OH; Springvale Country Club Ballroom, North Olmstead, OH; Columbia Ballroom, Columbia Station, OH; Cavana Ballroom, Cleveland, OH; Beachland Ballroom, Cleveland, OH; Lake Park Dance Pavilion, Coshocton, OH; The Aragon Ballroom, Chicago, IL; Trianon, Embassy, Holiday, Savoy, Lion's, Paladium, Green Mill, Vogue, Pison Park, Shutters Brothers, Majestic, Boulevard, Paradise, Boston Club and Allegro Ballrooms, Chicago; Blue Moon Ballroom, Aurora; Arcade Roof Gardens, Macomb-Roof Gardens, Galesburg; Ingleterra Ballroom, Peoria; Pioneer Gardens, Joliet; Indiana Oasis, Michigan City, IN; Palais Royale Ballroom, South Bend, IN' Madura's Danceland, Whiting; Midway Ballroom, Cedar Lake; Indiana Beach Ballroom, Monticello, IN; Edens Ballroom, Westchester, IN; Crystal Ballroom, Bass Lake; The Warehouse, Carter Lake, IA; Danceland, Cedar Rapids, IA; Modernistic Ballroom, German Hall, Shad Oak, Clinton, IA; Aronda, Creston, IA; Tromar Ballroom, Riviera Ballroom, Des Moines; Melody Mill, Dubuque; Gala Ballroom, Independence; Riviera Ballroom, Janesville; Armar Ballroom, Marion; Coliseum Ballroom, Oelwein; Prairie Moon, Prairieburg; Rigadoon, Tomba, Skylon Ballrooms, Sioux City, IA; Arnold's Park, Spirit Lake, IA; Cobblestone Ballroom, Storm Lake, IA: Rainbow Gardens, Waterville, IA; Ritz Ballroom, Trig Ballroom, New Moon Ballroom, Wichita, KS; Crystal Palace Ballroom, Coloma, MI; Graystone, Arcadia, Aragon, Campus, Eastwood Garden, Grand Terrace, New Danceland, Castle, Vanity, Crystal, Paw Paw Ballrooms, Detroit; The Bob-Lo Island Pavilion, Detroit; Manitov Beach Ballroom, Manitov Beach; Big Pavilion, Saugatuck; Shadowland Pavilion, St. Joseph; and Walled Lake Casino, Walled Lake, MI;

Terp Ballroom, Austin, MN; Marigold Ballroom, Minneapolis, MN; The Prom, St. Paul, MN; The Coliseum, Worthington, MN; El Torreon, LaFiesta, Pla Mor, Ballrooms, Kansas City, MO; Tunetown, St. Louis, MO; Owl's Roost, Arcadia, NE; State Ballroom, Bee, NE; Turnpike Ballroom, Lincoln, NE; Kings Ballroom, Norfolk, NE; Royal Terrace Ballroom, Omaha, NE; Oscar's Palladium, Sargent, NE; Mr. Tunes, Sioux City, NE; Froghop Ballroom, St. Joseph, NE; Casa Loma Ballroom St. Louis, NE; Moonlight Gardens, Canton, OH; Castle Farm, Moonlight Garden, Cincinnati, OH; Aragon Ballroom, Trianon Ballroom, Euclid Beach Ballroom, Puritas Springs Amusement Park Ballroom, Chipawa Ballroom, Circle Ballroom, Trianon Ballroom, Cleveland, OH; Maples Ballroom, Rootstown, OH; Continental Gardens, Akron, OH; Banater Hall, Lorain, OH; Homestead Ballroom, Lakewood, OH; Cinderella Ballroom, Appleton, WI; Wisconsin Roof Ballroom, WI; Dutch Mill, Lake Delaven, WI; Riviera Ballroom, Lake Geneva, WI

Far West Ballrooms

Rendezvous Ballroom, Balboa, CA; Chateau Ballroom, The Palomar, Los Angeles; Ali Babi Ballroom, Oakland, CA; Casino Gardens, Ocean Park, CA; Mission Beach Dance Casino, Pacific Square, San Diego, CA; Balconades/Wolohaus, The Pergola, Shalimar, Trianon/Primalon, Avalon, Palamara El Patio Ballrooms, San Francisco, CA; Aragon, Santa Monica, CA; Palladium, Hollywood, CA; Elitch Gardens, Rainbow, El Patio, Trocadero Ballrooms, Denver, CO; Miramar Ballroom, Boise, UT; El Patio Ballroom, Reno, NV; White Way Ballroom, Maud, OK; Gibson's Ballroom, Muskogee, OK; The Hippodrome,Oakmudge, Shawnee, OK; Cain's Ballroom, Tulsa, OK; Crystal Gardens Ballroom, Salem, OR; Roaring 20's, San Antonio, TX; Pleasure Pier, Galveston, TX; Rice Hotel, Houston, TX; Saltaire Amusement Park, Terrace Ballroom, Salt Lake City, UT; Abbey Ballroom, Tacoma, WA; Century Ballroom, Seattle, WA; Evergreen Ballroom, Olympia, WA; Leif Erickson Ballroom, Seattle, WA; Orion Ballroom, Kirkland, WA; Pacific Ballroom, Pacific, WA; Spanish Castle, Seattle/Tacoma, WA; Trianon Ballroom, Seattle, WA; Natatorium Ballroom, Spokane, WA; Century Ballroom, Tacoma, WA

Southern Ballrooms

Hotel Peabody, Casino Ballroom, Memphis, TN; Hotel Chase, New Orleans, LA; Flagler Gardens Ballroom, Miami, FL; Tybrisa Ballroom, Tybee Island, GA; Trocadero, Henderson, KY; Madrid Ballroom, Louisville, KY; Tantilla Ballroom, Richmond, VA; Seaside Park, Virginia Beach, VA; The Jekyll Island Convention Center, Jekyll Island, GA

Big Band

Road Warriors

He loved life and he loved his family and his music, too. That's why those who knew and followed bandleader Edmund George "Red" Sievers of Remsen, IA are still saddened by his untimely death on an October morning, 1941. He was 33 and just beginning to feel comfortable with the trumpet and his band of road warriors. He was a self-taught cornet player which made him commonplace in a day when musicians picked up instruments and began learning music on their own. His grandfather, George, also played the cornet and performed professionally for 20 years before he moved the family north to Wilmont, in southwest Minnesota where he entered the retail business. His grandfather knew when to get out of the work-a-day world, though, and enjoy life.

He retired to become a catfisherman and later a champion fisherman. He died in 1976, the second year of Jimmy Carter's presidency, at 92.

Red made his name synonymous with big band music in Minnesota early in his life. His younger sister Lindia, a teenager, sang with the Sievers' band and later married one of her brother's musicians, saxophonist Al Nichols, says Lindia's daughter Jill Bartlett. It was a musical family story similar to Guy Lombardo, Ray Anthony, the Dorsey brothers, Benny Goodman and a number of others. When one brother broke into the business, others followed.

It was a common thread among territorial bands to have brothers and sisters sit in and become regulars. Everyone from the big band era and those that followed always think of celebrity bandleaders when they talk about the music and the period but, in fact, it was the territorial bands where musicians frequently made their names and cemented friendships. In the 1920s, there were 900 dance orchestras and 7,200 musicians traveling the country making a living—or trying to—playing popular music for dancers.

Today, by Google count there are over 300,000 musicians struggling to survive in a business that has never offered any guarantees even when you're good. Said John Ghrist, who keeps big bands alive in Chicago at station WDCB on his program *Midwest Ballroom*, "Everyone likes the big bands. Young people actually get to see good and talented musicians playing their instruments in uniform fashion. What do the kids get out of seeing anything less? The parks and cities have forgotten about the big bands and seldom hire them for the

Bob Harry   Photo courtesy of Lou DiSario

seniors who remember this great music… Harry James was right, big bands never went away. They are just ignored by the young people who control all the media and local events." John is right, in my opinion. Music follows contemporary trends and one look at what is promoted today and you know that you'll only hear authentic big band music at occasional local concerts or dances or on your home CD player.

In the old days, territories were designated throughout the United States to help bands benefit from booking agencies. Red's band, for example, played in the Midwest where the territory was referred to as **MINK** which translated to Minnesota, Iowa, Nebraska and Kansas. The territory band desperately needed representation because of the bleak economy (the Depression) and the number of bands competing for a shrinking number of engagements. Said *Wikipedia* in describing the era: "While many territory bands were high quality, they rarely recorded and were often unfairly considered minor league compared to the national touring bands. Ambitious and hopeful young musicians saw territory bands as a training ground for, or rite of passage, to major touring bands. The alumni of territory band musicians who matriculated to fame within the industry reads like a 'who's who in music.'" At the same time, what musicians endured on their way was to some "indescribable." Musician and bandleader Lee Barron probably said it best when he told the Territory Bands Database "If anybody wrote a book about Territory Bands–nobody would believe it!" The conditions, the pay, their travel arrangements or lack of, their lack of a sound system of any kind and the hardships forced on women singers and black musicians were disgraceful from a 21st century perspective. But those who wanted to play tolerated them.

They played in open fields, hotels, restaurants, nightclubs, Elks Lodges, VFW halls, Grange halls, basement annexes, high school or college gymnasiums or field houses, warehouses, Quonset huts, armories, rooming house verandas, name it and a bandleader will tell you he played there. It was the nature of the business. For example, most of us who played have great stories about how we had to fit our instruments into nooks and crannies to play some gigs. We rarely had to spread out to cover space. I played a high school several times where the piano wasn't on the stage so the pianist and the bassist were on the floor of the auditorium while I was up on the stage with my drums along with the brass and woodwind sections.   I could have used a later day drum machine to give me the metronome beat in a headset (new technology not yet available then). Setting a tempo was a new experience with each number.

Location wasn't the only thing that could cause trouble for musicians, however. Heat, humidity and acoustics could cause you to tune your axe throughout the night. Few places like gyms, even country clubs were air-conditioned at the time. Even drums (the old cowhide heads, at least) needed adjustment.

But traveling the road was brutal, most musicians told me. Listen to Mel Torme, who in 1988 put down his reminisces of a life of traveling in his book, *Mel Torme: It Wasn't All Velvet*, Zebra Books, 1988. He got a gig at the Paramount Theater as an extra attraction with the Charley Spivak Orchestra, the featured performer. He

> *He was being paid $1,750 a week to open and he said that "by industry standards, that was lousy."*

was being paid $1,750 a week to open and he said that "by industry standards was lousy." Vic Damone was getting more and that was tension he didn't need. "Thereafter the struggle to increase my income was endless and terribly difficult," he wrote. After his marriage to Candy Toxson in Chicago, he made a hurried trip to NYC so he could open with the Buddy Rich Band at the Paramount. It was a difficult engagement. Buddy would end his set with a powerful and blazing drum solo leaving the crowd exhausted. Mel followed Buddy as some left for the bathroom or elsewhere.

While New York and Chicago were hubs because of media and the potential for larger audiences, the big band story was more diversified than many thought. "There was a huge number of excellent bands that rarely visited New York or Chicago; some never at all. They were based in smaller cities and often employed a fairly stable roster of sidemen. They were local musicians. They toured their area playing in cafes, ballrooms, vaudeville shows, school affairs, and such. Overall, they played a rather eclectic mix of classical, popular and ragtime music. While their local performances were rarely recorded, their playing was usually happy, lively and they supplied their audiences with reasonably high quality entertainment. Many of the bands were fully the equivalent of any of the nationally known or so-called 'name' bands," said Small Territory Bands Database.

But touring entertainers found a lengthy stay at a theater or hotel could have side effects. Ed Gabel, road manager for the Stan Kenton Band in his book *Stan Kenton: The Early Years: 1941-1947*, told of the boring and repetitive nature of long theater dates. The stage shows never varied. It was steady work, all agreed, but time lost all meaning. It was card games, more card games and waiting to go on and repeating the same thing the next day and the next.

The band business, however, was changing during the 1930s as leaders tried to find business methods to promote and make profitable what were hit or miss experiences. The Casa Loma band was probably the best investment a group of musicians made in themselves. Yet it was a risk, too. Bands came together by word of mouth and the leader, who usually was either from a wealthy family or was good at persuading people to support him financially, owned the music stands, probably the charts and quite possibly had use of his father's touring sedan. My "wheels" were a very good friend and tenor saxophonist named Jim Booker who got me to gigs with a complete Slingerland drum set stuffed in the trunk and back seat of his car.

The Casa Loma Orchestra formed in 1927 in Detroit as one of a number of swing bands. It incorporated in 1930, one of the few to take such a step. The members of the band were all stockholders and board members and it played under the title of *Orange Blossoms*, the name it took when it began. It had leaders like violinist Hank Biagini and later Glen Gray. The orchestra started cutting records two years before it incorporated. In describing the stock company, *Wikipedia* said: "The band members were hired on the grounds of 'musical and congenial' competence and follow strict conduct and financial rules. Members who broke the rules could be summoned before the 'board', have their contract bought out and be ejected from the band." Nothing like a band led by the majority of its stockholders!

The name Casa Loma came after an opening night that never happened. A Google search shows that Casa Loma is a popular name for developers in Canada. In the pre-1940s days, the band was scheduled to open a new nightclub in Canada. The opening was special because the Prince of Wales was expected to attend. But the club never served its first drink or opened its doors at the time. The band capitalized on the moment and decided the club name was appropriate for them, too.

A long term radio engagement with the Camel Caravan in the 1930s where it introduced its theme *Smoke Rings* gave the band plenty of promotion. The band's hits like *Casa Loma Stomp*, *No Name Jive*, and *Maniac's Ball* gave it added juice and notoriety especially on college campuses where it enticed collegians to the dance floor to very smooth and sophisticated music. Ironically, months later when Benny Goodman had his successful west coast tour in 1935 and put jazz on the American map, the Casa Loma Orchestra's star began to lose luster. In the 1940s, it was never again a pacesetter and stopped touring although it continued recording.

Years later, another band tried to replicate the Casa Loma success. Si Zentner, a staff musician who worked on such Hollywood film hits as *Singing in the Rain*, and *A Star Is Born* at MGM Studios, was determined to lead his own band like the Elgarts and Casa Loma. He got a contract with Liberty Records in 1959 as most big bands were selling off their charts and few band promoters were booking big musical groups. He staffed a full scale big band and took it on the road playing every college he could find and what nightclubs and ballrooms were left. According to his records, he played 178 one-nighters in a row which was a six month endurance test that even major bands like Goodman, James, Krupa, Kenton and even Woody Herman found fatiguing. While skeptics still thought his effort would fail, Zentner proved them wrong. His band, which featured the influence of groups he had worked with like Les Brown, Harry James and Jimmy Dorsey, won the Best Band in the *Downbeat* Readers poll 13 times! In 1961, he was chosen the best trom-

Hal Leonard Orchestra Trumpet Artist "EV" Photo courtesy of James Ronan Collection IA

Ralph Martiere Band   Photo courtesy of Chuz Alfred

bonist and his band won the *Playboy's Jazz Readers' Poll*. But even Zentner's positive exposure and results didn't last. In 1965, he moved from Los Angeles to Las Vegas to open the Tropicana's 500-seat lounge, the *Blue Room*, and back the popular Mel Torme. In 1968, he took a step away from the big bands and became the musical director of one of Vegas' longest running floor shows, *Folies Bergere*. Columnist Joe Delaney of the *Las Vegas Sun* said it best: "While trombonists were not known much for their longevity in the business, Si was an exception. He was even playing well to the end of his career." He battled the crippling disease leukemia during his final years but continued to play up to six months before his death.

But there were other worries musicians had the public never realized. For example, in cramped spaces you took the chance of having your mouthpiece bumped by other players because bandsmen did get up and move around on the stand. Some leaders, like Miller, Lionel Hampton, Woody Herman, Duke Ellington, Jimmy Lunceford and Count Basie among others thought the novelty of all the members of a section standing and wildly swinging their instruments back and forth and up and down added more excitement and novelty to uptempo pieces. But cut or bruised lips could put a player out of action for a night… even a career. Trombonists and trumpeters in Lunceford- influenced bands did lots of gyrations which meant moving their slides and horns in different directions. One 1940 film clip saw the baritone saxophonist in the Ralph Martiere band lying on his back holding his over sized sax with his feet and honking. The bigger problem was getting up!

Paul Tanner, who played trombone with the Glenn Miller Orchestra, said the guys always use to dread it when Glenn came back from watching the Lunceford band. "Glenn would want us to do some really athletic feats with the horns and it could be dangerous in the section," he said. After the war, Tex Beneke took over the reorganized Glenn Miller Orchestra with the approval of Glenn's wife Helen and Tex continued Glenn's fascination with musicians in motion. Watch a *Film Classics Big Bands* video about big bands and you'll see trumpets and trombones tossing their instruments up and catching and swinging them side to side on the Miller standard *In The Mood*. Sidemen in the band at the time included trumpeters Red Rodney, Clyde Hurley, Lee Knowles, Dale McMickle and Ray Anthony; Tanner, Al Mastren, and Frank D'Annolfo on trombones, Bassist Rollie Bundock, Richard Fisher on guitar, Chummy Macgregor on piano and drummer Jack Sperling.

Another touring band that used to feature trombones, trumpets and saxophones swinging to the beat was the Ray Anthony Band. Ray was apart of such showmanship years earlier when he was with Miller. He launched his first band the year after World War II ended with arrangements and instrumentation that sounded like the Miller band but his trumpet lead gave the group a different style. His months with Glenn had disagreements with the leader and Ray left to join Jimmy Dorsey. He organized an innovative sound with a trumpet, French horn, five saxes and a rhythm section a short time later. I talked to him in early 2000 and he told me that while the big band era was far too short, he continued by finding "new places to play and record. You had to be aware of what audiences were out there and how to appeal to them." He remembered his beginning in the band business with his family, the Antonini Orchestra in Cleveland, when he was 5. Ray Antonini (Anthony) and his brothers were part of the family enterprise. Later, his brother Leo, who played baritone sax, joined him when he formed his orchestra. Four years in the navy leading service bands in the Pacific like pianist Claude Thornhill and clarinetist Artie Shaw gave him good connections when he left the military for civilian life, said Lou DiSario who joined Ray on USO shows as an emcee and singer/dancer. "Ray was a dynamo on stage. He led the band with enthusiasm and it showed. It excited the crowds." One of the links in Ray's story was songwriter Johnny Mercer. He had sung with the Anthony group. Shortly after he formed his orchestra Ray signed with Johnny's up and coming recording company, Capitol. Ray emulated Harry James' trumpet but the band counted on the audience recognition of the Miller sound. He took the band a step further when he used shout phrases. Although Anthony found many Miller techniques important, the personalities of the two men were a contrast. Glenn grew up in a conservative Midwestern farm town with strong family values. He didn't shun attention but he was surprisingly shy for a bandleader and spent more time finding ways to promote the music his band played. He rewrote and reduced his musical hits so he could get more music on his radio shows with Chesterfield. Ray, by contrast, basked in the limelight and gained from his Hollywood friends. And he was successful.

During the 1950s while the band business continued to plummet, Ray found his niche with television by capitalizing on TV show theme songs. His version of *Peter Gunn* became a best selling single and later, he took the title song for the popular black and white law and order show of the day, *Dragnet*, and recorded it. He brought more life to his tours when he ignited the dance craze called the *Bunny Hop*. His public appeal was noted by the trade magazines and his band was voted the number one dance band in the country.

Anthony's band "that is the talk of America" lived up to its reputation according to thousands of bobbysoxers and dancers. Carolyn Walters Ziebell, while a teenager growing up in Ohio, has wonderful memories of such bands playing at Buckeye Lake, OH's ballrooms. "I especially remember Keely Smith and the Louie Prima Orchestra. And the great sounds of Ray Anthony…we would dance for hours and be soaking wet…but it was such fun! I loved it when he did the *Bunny Hop*. Everyone got into it." Road bands had to keep their spirits up as they went from gig to gig and night after night of big crowds, long bus rides, fatigue, little sleep and lots of stale food. It was a few years before pizza was a hit. It was summertime in America in the 1940s and '50s.

Red Sievers Band

Said Red Sievers' son Richard, a science teacher in Minnesota, "Dad used to play his trumpet all the time and drive everyone crazy in the small town when he was learning to play with all the noise but then later, he was so good he became the 'hot' trumpet player who we were so proud of." Red's death left his mother Molly Kathryn Sievers to raise Richard's sister Sandra Kay and him during the war years and later. "She was a loving and wonderful mother," Richard said, "and we never missed a meal growing up without a dad. I had to learn everything by myself but I didn't know what I was missing until I was older."

Red's band started in the early 1930s. His first theme song was "Easy to Love." When the band was playing Minneapolis he changed his theme to fit his new family: "My Blue Heaven" was the new theme after the birth of a baby boy.

"You know the way the song goes... Just Molly (my mother) and me (Red) and baby (Richard) makes three... We're so happy in my blue heaven. . ." his son says. "I remember seeing some of the original scores that my dad had for his performances. They were done in his hand with penciled musical sheets. I know a lot of them were his own arrangements—especially his solos. My mother always said that he could not abide a missed note or a sloppy beat and everything had to be precise."

While the band played the Marigold Ballroom in Minneapolis during the winter months, Red would team with popular Lawrence Welk and his band when they did a number of one nighters at the Charmot Ballroom in Omaha. Red sat in with the Welk group and remembered the story of how the polka-playing bandleader got his start in Omaha when he and his new manager, Vic Schroeder, formed a booking agency to promote bands throughout the Midwest and decided Omaha was much larger and more supportive than other cities. You needed a musicians' union card and Lawrence didn't have one. When he applied he was told he would have to wait for at least six months. Vic thought Lawrence knew the rule but unfortunately he didn't.

It put Lawrence back on the road driving thousands of miles to play endless numbers of one nighters. His wife Fern told him it might be a good time to get out of the business entirely. So Lawrence Welk, bandleader, became Lawrence Welk gentleman chicken farmer when he bought a five acre plot near Peony Park. Lawrence found the first six months in farming difficult which he said was made worse by his kindness to his friends. He would ask them to drop by and have a free chicken dinner or a free chicken or both with the family figuring they would buy some chickens. That didn't always happen.

Business was brisk... but there was little money coming in, Lawrence lamented later. He went back on the road and continued to petition the union for membership. Red's band, meanwhile, may have been one of those selected to open for Lawrence at the Chermont as bands rotated in and out of dancing spots. It was a common practice at the time. Lawrence's popularity continued to grow but not with union officials. Lawrence asked a friend to find out why he couldn't get a membership. The friend found that union leaders thought of Lawrence as a threat because they were all musicians too. If Lawrence got a union card he would capitalize on his popularity at their expense. In 1938, Lawrence finally gave up his dream for success in Omaha and began looking elsewhere. Pittsburgh, for example, was interested in the Welk group and it was there that fan mail suggested his music was "sparkly and bubbly" and the band began playing "champagne music." Lawrence put the words together and wrote his theme *Bubbles in the Wine*.

One-nighting with Lawrence was always fun, band members said. In the 1940s, Joan Mowery, the band singer, remembers Lawrence used to tell his bus audience who lived in various farmhouses as they drove by. Finally, Joan quipped, "I said Lawrence why don't you stop kidding us. You don't really know these people. Lawrence pulled into the next driveway at a farm near Hooper, NE. The owner was milking a cow. The farmer insisted the band stay for breakfast. The band ended up staying for a typical Nebraska farm dinner as well." Lawrence smiled satisfied he had made his point.

Although he promised to return to Omaha, Lawrence never did. He went on to live in Chicago and then the west coast. In the band business, many said, you just kept moving on hoping the next engagement would be better. Years later, Leo McElroy, part-time announcer and TV reporter for CBS, NBC, PBS and ABC recalls what a Lawrence Welk Saturday night telecast was like. "Doing Welk didn't take much skill. I intro'd the maestro, got off the stage, grabbed a bite to eat (free!) and was back on stage in time to sign off. I got to do the half-hour pickup of Welk from the Hollywood Palladium. Then while colleague Dick Sinclair did the 10 p.m. pickup of Freddy Martin from the Coconut Grove of the Ambassador Hotel, I drove like hell to Glendora (a far Los Angeles outskirt) to do the 11 p.m. of Johnny Catron's big band from the Glendora Palms —the best live music of my evening! I intro'd the numbers and was up with the band throughout. It was much more fun! We did that Saturday night gig for a couple of years," he wrote me.

Meanwhile, the Sievers band was working similar territory in the Midwest and lining up return engagements to make travel worthwhile during stressful times.

It all came to an end just two months before the world felt the shock of the Japanese attack on Pearl Harbor in 1941. The band was in Red's sleeper trailer, a trailer-truck design credited to Lawrence Welk, the first one to use it. They had finished a gig in Marshalltown, IA a few hours earlier and were headed back to Minneapolis. Thirteen miles north of Albert Lea, MN on Highway 65, a cattle truck was weaving back and forth as a driver tried to stay awake. The truck crossed the center line and collided with the band truck/trailer going in the opposite direction. The trailer was split in half and ironically six musicians on one side survived the crash but the six on the other were killed. The force of the crash threw many of the victims into a nearby field, including Red.

Jimmy Barnett & His Orchestra   Photo courtesy of James Ronan Collection, IA

Those were the dangers territorial bands faced in the early days of the 1920s and '30s on poor, usually unlit main roads and even more dangerous side roads that today would have been considered partially paved paths. Most bands traveled at night and early morning on lonely stretches of highways where not only were the roads poor and filled with potholes, the drivers of the cars and buses had played most of the evening and were not in condition to drive 6 to 10 or more hours. But, they would tell you, there was no other way since they usually had day jobs they had to get to in distant places.

Said *Wikipedia* in an excellent analysis of the scene: "Beginning in the 1920s, the bands typically had 8 to 12 musicians. These bands typically played one-nighters, 6 to 7 nights a week at venues like VFW halls, Elks lodges, Lions Clubs, hotel ballrooms, and the like. Many historians give much credit to territory bands for popularizing modern ballroom dancing that began during the World War I era with the influence of Vernon and Irene Castle."

They were part of Americana that's been forgotten and ignored today. Sadly, their contributions haven't been recognized. Again *Wikipedia* offers the best summation: "Territory bands helped disseminate popular music—which included swing, jazz, sweet dance music or any combination thereof—bringing it to remote gin mills and dance halls that were otherwise ignored by national booking agents representing genuine recording stars like Ellington and Armstrong. Even if jazz supremacists blanch at the comparison of other ensembles' hits. But many developed original repertoires and signature sounds, none more storied than Walter Page's Blue Devils, the Oklahoma City-based outfit that Count Basie joined in 1926."[1]

The intrigue and thrill of starting your own band continued even when the venues were mostly gone. The challenge, of course, came quickly when lack of money, people and no work faced every would-be bandleader. Listen to Alan Glasscock of Dallas, TX who has been working in the business since the 1980s. "The whole reason I decided to form a big band was because at that time, there were so-called 'big' bands (9-12 pieces) playing locally, but they didn't play 'real' big band music. I had been collecting the original big band recordings for several years… and none of the local big bands sounded like the recordings." His curiosity led him to launch his own big band and play "true" big band music. When he found he couldn't acquire charts he started taking lessons in arranging and began transcribing the charts from the original recordings. "The real challenge among many was learning to recognize what types of voicings I was hearing and translating them to paper," he remembers.

The Alan Glasscock Orchestra

Photo courtesy of Alan Glasscock

Equally challenging, he recalls, was finding musicians. "I had no long-term bookings and the initial group of musicians I pulled together was basically community band sorts. We played for a monthly dance held by a big band dance club in which I was a co-founder and we sounded pretty bad. At some point a few months into our existence, a local nursing home heard about us and offered to pay us a small fee to come and play for their residents. Other outside bookings came in and then I was faced with my biggest problem. I had to decide if I wanted to continue leading a band as a hobby or as a true business.

I opted for the business end of it." Then the pain began, he explained.

"I knew the only way to improve the sound and quality of my band was to cull out the weaker players and replace them with musicians more adequately suited for their chairs. Once we started receiving paying gigs, I quickly found out that 'money talks' and I could basically hire any musician in the area so long as I was able to pay them close to or above the going rate at the time."

Like many other leaders, whether touring or territorial, it was a "hard first lesson." Separating friendships and personal feelings from business logic isn't musical… it's necessary for survival. But Alan's experiences have all the ingredients of success. The similarity to Glenn Miller's time demonstrates how little if anything has changed. In Miller's day there were flamboyant bandleaders and bands.

Lucky Millender, Gene Krupa led such groups along with others. Miller, the Dorseys and Harry James led well orchestrated, swinging bands with exceptional talent and creative arrangements. Alan knows his strength. "I am pleased to be able to stand in front of some tremendous musicians of which I am in awe. My strong suit is arranging and it's a gift that I never realized until some 10 to 15 years ago," he told me. His work is recognized by his peers, too.

He's done arranging for the Glenn Miller Orchestra, the Grammy Award winning Manhattan Transfer and he works with Lush Life Music.

He's committed and dedicated to being a big band leader in an era when the term "big band" has little meaning. These days, big bands can actually mean big amplifiers and sound systems.

But he senses the grueling nature of the "work" leaders and bands had from the beginning to the end of the 20st century. Just getting to the gig was challenging in those pioneering days.

Typical road warriors were members of the Harry James in the 1940s Like nearly every band of that day Harry and his "Music Makers" spent time on the highways when it definitely wasn't fun. They remember when money was tight but Harry would come back to the bus sporting a new shirt and coat and he'd tell them that "the leader has to look good." They liked Harry so they took it in a good natured way. Bandsmen also remember when Harry was supposedly staying a step ahead of a repro man trying to take the band bus back to Greyhound because Harry had missed a payment. The band would pull into a hotel parking lot and scan the area for police or people checking license plates. Sometimes, the band would park on off-streets a block away to avoid scrutiny.

Then the James band did a CBS radio show with airchecks that brought raves about the Music Makers on the west coast. All of a sudden Harry was fronting one of America's most popular bands. *Variety* magazine carried a story describing how the James' band was making $12,500 a week at New York City's popular Paramount. The doors of the theater opened at 9:45 each morning and observers said that crowds began lining up at 5 a.m. Extra police were called to prevent a riot. The James band broke crowd records at both Frank Dailey's *Meadowbrook* on the east coast and the *Hollywood Palladium* on the west coast. Veteran trumpet player and arranger Neal Hefti told an album liner writer that "I played the *Palladium* twice with Harry James, twice with Woody Herman, twice with Charley Spivak and once with Ziggy Elman—all good solid bands—and nobody drew more than Harry." James and his musicians were crowned the band of the year in 1942 on Martin Block's *Make Believe Ballroom* taking the title from the country's best, Glenn Miller.

I heard the James Orchestra in the last year of the decade after he had left traveling for some months. What I loved about the band and others did too was the solid beat that came from drummers like Davey Tough, Ralph Hawkins, Jackie Mills, Mickey Scrima and, of course, Buddy Rich. An old time circus drummer before he picked up the trumpet, Harry had a sense of the beat that was exceptional. Dancers thoroughly enjoyed the two and four beat rhythm and overflow crowds demonstrated it. Trumpet player Ron Armstrong of upstate New York was a longtime devotee of James, his playing style and his persona. Ron passed away with a large collection of James' recordings which he said were examples of the quality of his trumpet, his terrific band and his style. "Listen to Harry play trumpet, pick up the bongos and shout encouragement to the band, he was a REAL bandleader. As a trumpet player I thought he was a stylist who could use and control vibrado with the best of them. And there were a number of good ones in his day."

Harry had quality sidemen who in many cases stayed with him for years. There were saxophonist Dave Matthews, tenor saxophonist Corky Corcoran, trombonist Ray Sims, older brother of Zoot, bassist Thurman Teague, heart throb vocalist Frank Sinatra and young girl singer Connie Haines.

One of the veteran musicians with the band for years was Rome, NY native, Jack Palmer. He was the kind of trumpet player who could solo and play behind Harry with ease. Jack spent his playing years in New York City with some of the best in the business at the time which included Red Norvo, Louis Armstrong, Tommy Dorsey, Glen Miller, Benny Goodman, Artie Shaw, Count Basie and Mildred Bailey. A skilled player, he read music at a time when a number of musicians didn't. Therefore, he was able to join Sammy Spears who had a studio band playing for the hit shows *The Honeymooners* and *The Jackie Gleason Variety Show*. Jack took over the Bunny Berigan group for a time before he returned to his hometown and opened a restaurant named appropriately the Palmer House.

Another road veteran was William "Count" Basie, a guy who was content to play all night long in Kansas City clubs just to have gigs. He got his break when an experimental radio station aired the Basie band in December, 1936, and the program was heard in Chicago. Wealthy jazz enthusiast John Hammond caught the band and told Benny Goodman about the music. Benny, who had been discovered by John, passed the message on to his booker Willard Alexander. Willard was willing to give the band a chance even though George Simon, the legendary band critic, wasn't as supportive. Wrote George: "True, the band does swing, but that sax section is so invariably out of tune. And if you think that sax section is out of tune, catch the brass! And if you think the brass by itself is out of tune, catch the intonation of the band as a whole! Swing is swing, but music is music. Here's hoping the outfit sounds better in person." The Count, who was born in Red Bank, NJ not Kansas City, had taken on the task of putting together a band from a reorganization of the Bennie Moten group in 1935 when Benny died. Basie took members of the Moten organization and formed what he called *Count Basie and his Barons of Rhythm*. Bill Basie showed his flair for innovation when he used two tenor saxophones—one of them the great Lester Young—to duel, a novelty at the time. Woody Herman would later use the technique to form the throaty Four Brothers sax section that featured two tenors.

The rhythm section was given emphasis and the Basie sound was born. When anyone heard him, they couldn't get over the simplicity. "Here's a cat plinking on the piano with one hand and people love'd it," said one enthusiastic Basie fan. Within a year, Basie's indelible sound became a trademark which drew crowds and helped create the hit that identified the band; *One O'Clock Jump*.

"We hit it with the rhythm section and went into the riffs and the riffs just stuck. We set the thing up front in D-flat and then we just went on playing in F," the Count later explained. His popularity exploded. He took the band on a whirlwind cross-country tour that included the West Indies.

When they returned to New York again he set up headquarters at an obscure place called the Woodside Hotel (it explains the other Basie hit called *Jumpin' at the Woodside*). The band practiced in the hotel basement and then scored again with a gig that showcased his new sound at the *Roseland Ballroom.* Hammond helped energize the Basie image when he brought sexy black vocalist Billie Holiday to the band and they opened at the revered *Apollo Theatre.* The Count continued to enhance the Basie sound introducing Eddie Durham as his composer and arranger and vocalist Jimmy Rushing. He added drummer Jo Jones, saxophonists Buddy Tate, Tad Smith and Lester Young, bassist Walter Page, guitarist Freddie Green, trumpeters Buck Clayton, Harry Edison and trombonists Vic Dickenson and Dickie Wells to headline all-star shows.

I saw the Basie band in the 1950s in Columbus after the band had popularized the smash hit *April In Paris* and the rave response, "one more time!" Count Basie was one of a kind and he proved it with every road trip…

And you can't talk about road warriors without including Edward Kennedy "Duke" Ellington. He spent more than 50 years traversing the United States and he took his band all over the world "loving everyone… madly!"

Duke didn't call his music jazz he said because, he told media, it was "American music." It didn't have a category, he added, noting that it was played by some greats in their own right.

And he made his band feel apart of his many pieces of music by featuring any number of his sidemen. There was alto saxophonist Johnny Hodges who Duke singled out with his composition *Jeep's Blues*, trumpeter Cootie Williams who stood out on Duke's *Do Nothing Til You Hear From Me*, Tricky

Russell's Danceland on Oneida Lake Photo courtesy of Jack Henke

Sam Nanton and Bubber Miley who were featured on the great Ellington hit, *The Mooche*. He brought songs written by sidemen to the public's attention, too. Ellington introduced the mood setting music called the *Spanish*

Tinge when he played Juan Tizol's *Caravan* and *Perdido*.

Where did the title "Duke" come from? His mother Daisy's friends and a neighborhood buddy Edgar McEntree created his royalty. Daisy's friends said young Edward had a "casual, offhanded manner, his easy grace and his dapper dress gave him the bearing of a young nobleman." It was Edgar who called him "Duke."

Big band enthusiasts who happened to live on the "the big band trail" from New York City or Boston west heard, felt and danced to hundreds of groups over the decades of the 30s and 40s. Utica, NY, was on that caravan westward even though events were held in a panorama that included ballrooms, armories, large restaurants and a theater. Miller and his band visited the Mohawk Valley in the late 1930s and they appeared at three spots; the Stanley Theater, the Mohawk Armory and Russell's Danceland outside of Sylvan Beach on Oneida Lake. Glenn probably wanted to forget that first visit. It came on the tail end of an aborted swing upstate that was hit by snowstorms, breakdowns and poor crowds and finished nearly broke. Glenn folded the band New Year's Eve, 1937. A year later, with band booker Irv Shribman's financial support and players like saxophonists Hal McIntyre and a young singing Texan named Beneke dubbed "Tex," the "new" Miller sound and orchestra set the music world on fire. In months, Miller catapulted to more fame than any band of the time and appearances at the Glen Island Casino, New Rochelle, on the banks of Long Island sound must have given Glenn great satisfaction after earlier days of frustration. When NBC kicked off its 1939 season, he went from making a net of about $24 a month to grossing over $700,000 by the autumn of 1940!

Gunther Schuller in his excellent review of the period *The Swing Era: The Development of Jazz 1930-1945 (The History of Jazz, Vol 2)*, contended that territory bands "by definition, were black. There were, of course, many white bands in the 'territories' but they tended to have the more lucrative and permanent jobs and therefore not required to travel as much as the black bands."

His point is arguable because as my research shows white bands were involved in the same struggle for survival. Black bands could count on something that white bands never seemed to have; places to stay in the communities for little or nothing. Yes, black musicians found motels and rooming houses closed to them because of their race but their extended families and the loving relationship black families had with musicians of the time tell a different story. White musicians, meanwhile, had to pay their way in motels, boarding houses and cottages on the inland lakes in middle America and coastal resorts. Both groups of musicians were clearly road warriors in a day when travel and pay were hardly the best.

During my playing days in the late '40s and early '50s in several white collegian territorial bands and a society band we didn't have "lucrative and permanent" jobs unless you count day labor in a dairy bar or clerking at a military surplus store at wages far lower than today's minimum. Worse, there were times in the college orchestras we didn't get paid at all. If the crowd was light, some proprietors made it clear we weren't going to get anything... We had no contracts nor did we have the resources to get legal help. We were transient workers not the community's stellar citizens. Worse, ballroom and club owners knew we were pickup bands put together on the spur of the moment or a few days. Before Social Security was enacted in 1935, there was little accountability of band members. Leaders told me they picked up or lost players hours before gigs and the "show had to go on."

However, most territory bands---whether black, white, integrated, male, female— were nearly always paid, *Wikipedia* said. Neither the booking agencies nor the musicians got rich, but regular salaries helped maintain pretty decent musicianship. Unfortunately, few if any territory bands had "regular" salaried people... including the leader, I discovered. Why the discrepancies? Lack of work and little documentation.

That's one of the reasons the National Orchestra Service (NOS) came into existence from the 1930s to the 1960s. Bands on either coast had the benefit of clubs, ballrooms and other places to play. But those in the midlands of the country struggled to be known, find gigs and keep their organizations together.

The NOS specialized in booking bands that featured ballroom dancing and orchestras with the Glenn Miller sound. The organization was head-quartered in Omaha and booked gigs in Wisconsin, Minnesota, North and South Dakota, Montana, Wyoming, Nebraska, Missouri, Kansas, Oklahoma and on military bases.

The music business wasn't organized, the union in the early years wasn't strong and so many players dropped in and out of the business. Musicians were, said one club owner, "a dime a dozen and sometimes too independent. Owners and bookers had control of the market. Territorial musicians frequently weren't paid a reasonable rate because some markets had too many bands." But those who played accepted it as the price it took to be in a band and playing...somewhere.

Some of the bands managed by NOS were Verne Byers, Chan Chandler, Jerry Mosher, Del Clayton, Wayne Chapman, John Paul Jones Orchestra, Al Hudson, Red Perkins & his Dixie Ramblers, Larry Elliott, Lee Williams, Mickey Bride, Nat Towles, Anna Mae Winborn and the Cotton Club

Boys, Little John Beecher, Jack Russell and his Sweet Rhythmic Orchestra, Earl Gardner and his Orchestra and Bob Calame and his Music.

Williams was a smart businessman/leader. While touring for a half-year, he would book the second half then "sell" the band and take the months off he wanted. In 1952, he became a partner in NOS. Towles, a black leader, was one of the best bands in the NOS stable, observers said. Winborn, also black, was one of the few women on the road fronting a reputable band.

Today's bandleaders acknowledge their 20th century predecessors and the hardships of their road experiences but the pain today is still there; lack of money, time restrictions which force leaders to spend more effort organizing and scouring their regions for quality personnel never seem to end. Listen to Gordon Goodwin, leader of the *Big Phat Band*, which caught the public's attention in the early part of 2000. "I am fortunate to have access to people who share my belief that the big band genre can be contemporary, vibrant and alive. It can also be a huge pain in the keister. Organizing 18 busy schedules for gigs and recording sessions and taking those same 18 guys on the road, away from their families is a real challenge. Trying to market this kind of music in our current pop-culture environment is equally a task. There are a lot of reasons not to attempt an endeavor like this. So why am I doing it? I can't answer for everybody but for me, it's because the sound of a good big band is unique in all music. It can be powerful, visceral and exciting. It can also be tender, gentle or humorous and entertaining. At its best, it combines the structure of composition with the spontaneity of improvisation. The music I write for this band pushes these musicians to excel at a high level. There's a strong commitment to ensemble playing in this band, as we strive for the level of teamwork and nuance you hear from the best bands of the past. Yet, when each steps forth, his dedication to the art of improvisation is clear as well."

Joe Enroughty, another 21st century bandleader, believes that promoting an orchestra has become easier than the early days of the business. The Internet has opened a vast world of possibilities. "I maintain a large e-mail list and promote many

Johnny Whitney and His Orchestra   Photo courtesy of James Ronan Collection, IA

of our public performances that way. Facebook has also become a very useful tool, helping us tap into the younger demographic. Our web site is also a good marketing tool. On the web site we have sound samples, video clips and more information about the orchestra. The site www.guylombardomusic.com generates interest.

Of course, printing good old fashioned flyers is still an option and a very useful one for those who have yet to migrate to the Internet. For every public performance I generally print well over 200 flyers and usually hand out or post each and every one of them."

While a number of bandleaders think the business is sliding backward, Joe says "the band business has certainly improved since I began my orchestra in 2004. Part of this may be due to the fact that I am starting to make a name for myself. When you're a nobody, nobody wants to hire you. But we've built up a reputation around the area and we're well known as a top notch, first class orchestra now. We've traveled to Washington, DC, area to perform, we've appeared on television and radio and we've also been featured in several books and Internet publications. We were even asked to perform a wedding reception in Great Britain (we had to turn it down because of the high cost of travel). I try to carry all of my 'local' musicians with me whenever we play out of town. This keeps the orchestra sounding as good out of town as it does in town. Guy Lombardo never used to use 'pick-up' musicians and I don't like to do it either."

Road warriors don't fade away… they keep playing and playing… and playing. Says Enroughty: "I don't plan to stop playing anytime soon."

1. To find out more about the territorial bands read the Territory Bands Database online at www.nfo.net/territor/index.html

Society Orchestras

Sweet Sounds Were Very Successful

Music critic George T. Simon dismissed them as "Mickey Mouse" bands and even refused to review some during his days writing columns and magazine stories. Yet, a good number of successful dance bands from the 1930s until the end of the big band era were called "society orchestras."

To George, the "Mickey Mouse" bands were mostly in the Midwest and he found them inferior to what he felt were the "real" orchestras of the day. "For some reason that may be related to the section's inherent conservatism, bands that phrased in an old-fashioned way and blazed few new trails found ready acceptance, " he wrote in his popular book *The Big Bands*. "Most of these bands were led not by first-rate musicians but by businessmen, many of whom were top-flight executives who knew how to keep their mechanical men operating at maximum efficiency," he added.

The problem with George's standards, of course, was that the public was interested in music they could understand, easily enjoy and dance to and not all bandleaders understood that or wanted to abide by such a restriction. Simon thought that such orchestras were best suited for dance parties. Yet, most of them were hired routinely for ballroom dances, too. To the average bobbysoxer and crewcut of the era if the song had a melody, a good dance beat and you were among friends at a gathering place everybody knew and enjoyed, the fun already had begun. The music, though, had to be danceable.

According to the web site www.societyorchestras.com there were two types of society bands. One was considered "band agencies" and the other were independent bands.

The Band Agencies were orchestras playing various gigs the same night under the same name. Meyer Davis, for example, had 10 different bands playing the same night at 10 different sites.

The independent bands were usually booked by hotels where they played dance music for audiences. They also picked up gigs to play parties, holiday events and private balls and galas. Eddie Duchin and his Orchestra was considered one of the most popular but others grew in image too. Gimmick sounds made some stand out. For example, Grey Gordon used temple blocks to create a clock ticking and he named his group Grey Gordon and his Tick Tock Rhythm. Another successful entrepreneur bandleader was Shep Fields who had a sideman blow bubbles through a straw in a glass of water and called his band Shep Fields and his Rippling Rhythm. Lawrence Welk and his musicmakers used the popping of a champagne cork and bubbly sounds to add effects mid-20th century.

River Edge, Alexandria Bay, NY   Photo courtesy of Behrens Family Archive

Some musicians who thought themselves "hip" and "groovy" and on the cutting edge of the business despised so-called "sweet bands." A number considered themselves superior in technique and ability to those in such orchestras. The irony was that many career big band musicians were forced sometime during their playing years to become members of such bands if they wanted to keep working. Like most professions, musicians wanted to believe that what they created was important and of value especially to their peer group. The public, however, saw it for what it was – entertaining, depending upon your tastes, nothing more. Trombonist Kenny Trimble, who I saw with Stan Kenton, was a fine musician who reached the pinnacle of success when he was with Kenton. Yet, years later, I noted he was a trombonist with Lawrence Welk, a novelty bandleader Kentonites scorned during the 1950s. Trimble must have realized that Welk offered security and steady work at a time when many road bands, including Kenton's, were out of business or not traveling much.

Who were the sweet dance bands of the period? According to Simon, they included Blue Barron, Del Courtney, Emil Coleman, Chuck Foster, Jan Garber, Gray Gordon, Ev Hoagland, Art Kassel, Orville Knapp, Lester

Lanin, Meyer Davis, Ernie Hecksher, Ben Selvin and Tommy Tucker. He could have added Orrin Tucker, Tommy's brother; Sammy Kaye, Frankie Masters, Skinnay Ennis, Vaughn Monroe, Eddie Howard, Dick Jurgens, Leighton Noble, Will Osborne, Rudy Vallee, Carl Ravazza, Seger Ellis, Zinn Arthur, Bob Allen, Mitchell Ayers, Emery Deutsch, Al Donahue, Enoch Light, Eric Madriguera, Joe Venuti, Charlie Baum, Nat Brand-wynne, Carmen Cavallaro, Jack Fina, Johnny Green, Skitch Henderson, Claude Hopkins, Henry King, Wayne King, Vincent Lopez, Jay McShann, the half-Latin, half-society band Pancho, Joe Reichman, Freddie Slack, Ted Straeter, Frankie Carle, Teddy Wilson, Bob Zurke, Ted Lewis, Ted Weems, Johnny Bothwell, Georgie Auld, Sam Donahue and Carl "Deacon" Moore. Of course, there were others. A number of big band fans would always add Kay Kyser to such a list. They would enthusiastically say there was only one Kay Kyser.

His band was part society, part commercial and even part swing. And it certainly was part novelty. He copied other leaders yet he pioneered, too. For example, Kay featured singing song titles after hearing the same technique used by Sammy Kaye and Blue Barron. In 1941, Kay and his band were the first to play for military personnel something that he did often during the war years. His southern drawl and his engaging personality were his drawing cards. Consequently, he would join in singing and dancing with his orchestra and singing group, *The Honeydreamers*. Basically, like Cab Calloway, Harriet and Ozzie Nelson and Spike Jones, Kay was an entertainer as well as a bandleader. "Kay was a (real) businessman. We all liked him and liked what he stood for. He was first class. It's sad to say, but there are an awful lot of people who don't remember Kay Kyser," said his singer Harry Babbit.

He took his band and entourage to Hollywood and they appeared in a number of war movies. The band and Georgia Carroll, a blonde model and actress who became Mrs. Kay Kyser, appeared in *Yankee Doodle Dandy* and a year later, *Carolina Blues*. The Kyser Orchestra also appeared in the movie *Thousands Cheer*. Ginny Simms sang with the band for awhile but her own acting and singing careers took her elsewhere. The Kysers were a show business icon, remaining married until death took him in July, 1985.

During the war years, Kay joined the Church of Christ Scientist which some believe occurred because conventional medicine (his mother and father were both pharmacists) didn't help his severe arthritis problems. He told some he wanted to retire after the war but he continued until 1950.

Kay's fame however, is thought to have come from the program he devised to highlight every performance. It was a crowd pleaser and fit the fun-loving bandleader who would start each with his famous line, *"Evenin' folks, how y'all?"* His College of Musical Knowledge in which he starred as the Ol' Perfessor and would draw laughs from the simple line, "That's right…you're wrong!" The act was part musical, part quiz and including some singing. He had a number of sidemen who helped add the comedic side to the show. Cornet player Ish Kabibble, Sully Mason, Mike Douglas (who went on to his own career as a TV talk show host) and others were featured from time to time.

Certainly one of the leaders of the sweet band group was Guy Lombardo. Guy and his Royal Canadians crossed Lake Erie to play a Cleveland gig in 1925 and, while there and struggling financially, the band found a Chicago club that appeared interested in them. So anxious to find better money, Guy jumped at the move only to discover that the Grenada Café, the club that hired the band, was a front for the Chicago mob. The Canadians spent a few months playing for a nearly empty dance floor before Guy, desperate to get larger audiences, persuaded the management of radio station WBBM to do radio remotes of his Royal Canadians. Remotes were the rage at the time but Guy had to put in $75 of the $100 charge to convince a reluctant mob boss it was worthwhile. The results were far greater than Lombardo's wildest dreams. The exposure brought large crowds to the small café and relieved his sense of insecurity. Guy got nervous when he discovered that the café had a shooting gallery downstairs and a cemetery across the street. Months later, the remotes helped him land a gig with New York City's Roosevelt Grill. The Lombardo band parlayed the Roosevelt Grill contract into a lifetime of playing *Auld Lang Syne* every new year's eve in New York City

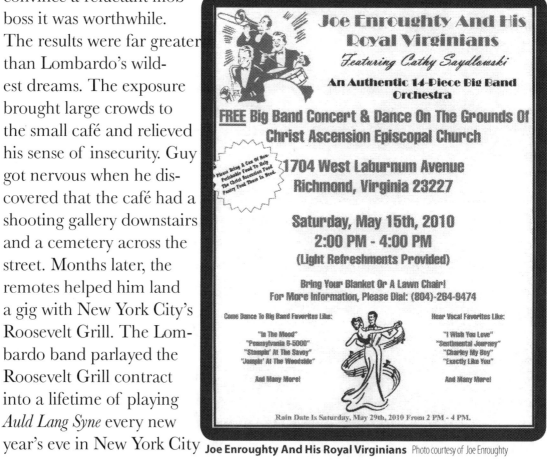

Joe Enroughty And His Royal Virginians Photo courtesy of Joe Enroughty

for millions on radio and television. And it went on for 33 years! While the official Lombardo band continues to play gigs, I think Guy would have been intrigued and inspired by a youthful 21st century bandleader whose band recreates the sound and attracts crowds. Thirty-two-year-old Joe Enroughty was fascinated by the Royal Canadian sound and modeled his orchestra, *The Royal Virginians*, to play the style as well as the old hits. Joe explains: "I have always been a big fan of the saxophones doubling on various instruments. We feature two alto saxophones, one tenor, and

one baritone. The two altos double on flute and clarinet. The tenor doubles on clarinet. And the baritone doubles on soprano saxophone, clarinet and bass clarinet. This gives the orchestra lots of tonal color."

His brass section uses a variety of mutes, including one that Tommy Dorsey made famous, to offer texture and depth for other numbers. "We use a tuba in place of a string bass because this is the essential that makes a sweet orchestra 'sweet.'" Joe continues. "When you take away the tuba, you change the entire style of the band. You should always adapt the song to fit your style rather than vice versa."

Joe follows the tradition of the bands of the 20th century by including "boy" and "girl" singers. Cathy Saydlowski and Dick Orange complete his 15 piece orchestra. "Dick performs a lot of Frank Sinatra material like *My Way*, *I've Got You Under My Skin* and *All the Way*." Yet, Joe says that they're not interested in duplicating a Sinatra recording. "We adapt those songs to our own style which I think makes it more creative." Cathy sings many of the band's ballads and Latin numbers and she also handles some of the country and western flavored arrangements. For a territory band, Joe takes authencity beyond what many others do. "We are constantly adding new arrangements to our library. We carry almost 200 charts on any given dance engagement and can typically handle just about any request. Our chief arranger is Steve Cooper of Chicago. He writes most of our charts for us because he understands our style and can recreate that sound on paper. We have about five different arrangers across the country who write for us and Steve we think is one of the best."

The band's versatility is it's strength. "We perform a wide variety of music from *Jumpin' At the Woodside* to *Anything Goes*. We have Dixieland numbers, swing and plenty of Latin selections, too. There's something for everybody and we get a lot of requests for waltzes and tangos."

Typically, Joe continues, the band performs at its share of weddings, private parties and corporate functions. But the band also plays for public gatherings too. "They are the most fun. I love it when people walk by and hear the music and just stop right where they are and start dancing. Young and old alike tend to do this. It's nothing to see grandma dancing with grandkids and a few baby boomers behind them tapping their feet to our music."

Ohioans seemed to enjoy the sweet, soft sounds of a North Carolina farm boy who played violin. Johnny Long, who grew up outside of Charlotte, joined with 10 other Duke University freshmen to launch the *Duke Collegians* and at the same time start his big band career. A likeable front man, Johnny and his friends stayed together during their college years and when they graduated, they renamed themselves *The Johnny Long Orchestra*. They toured and recorded under the Decca label and one recording made them popular at high school proms and college socials, *In A Shanty in Old Shanty Town*. In 1937, they released their first 78 for Vocalion Records called *Just Like That*. Two years later thanks to Long's promotional endeavors the band went on the *Fitch Summer Bandwagon Show*.

At Buckeye Lake, Long was a popular leader who led a band customized for dancing with his slogan "The Man Who's Long On Music." "It was always a smooth kind of band and you enjoyed dance after dance. I remember his theme about Shanty Town and I also remembered *My Dreams Are Getting Better All the Time*," said one Johnny Long enthusiast. In April, 1941, he and his band were selected to play for President Franklin D. Roosevelt's Birthday Ball. The band also backed popular singer Ella Fitzgerald on her recording of *Confessin' That I Love You*. At the same time, the orchestra made its first movie appearance with Abbott & Costello in *Hit the Ice* where bandleader Long played the romantic lead opposite singer Ginny Simms.

On the local level there were more sweet bands than jazz bands for a good reason. If you wanted to be hired by the country club, Elks Club or any social group, you had to have good dance charts. It wasn't much different at the touring level, really. Benny Goodman, for example, was considered the "King of Swing" but when he played college or major dances his book was filled with melodic dance music, too. It had to be. The leader of the society band I played with fashioned his group as a Glenn Miller-style band and, as such, he played sets of dance number after dance number and would end a set with a swing number, normally a two-beat Dixie piece. *Sister Kate* came up frequently. When people want to dance, Lombardo said, they don't have "to be held captive by the band."

Goodman had a number of terrific jazz musicians, Fletcher Henderson's swing arrangements and there were calls for some of them everywhere he went. Yet, he knew the consequences of disappointing an audience of dancers by playing *Don't Be That Way* or *Sing, Sing, Sing* most of the evening. In those days, a hard core number loved fast dancing but the majority who went to the floor didn't want to embarrass themselves either. Fast danc-

The Jo-Kar at Lancaster, OH - Dancing Spot   Photo courtesy of Behrens Family Archive

ing took considerable energy and gyrations that some felt awkward doing. Thus, Benny played plenty of sweet numbers. Obviously, musicians didn't necessarily like such a program because rarely did a slow number carry a drum solo or feature other players doing long extemporaneous selections. Compared to other bands on the road, there were few sidemen who took long solos on the Glenn Miller band either. Some suggested that the tightly arranged compositions, written in strophic form helped create the successful musical blend. It was a combination of the same phrase and chord structure repeated a number of times. Miller studied it and saw the value… and so did others. But he was a master at making sure the music the audience wanted to hear and dance to was what they heard. He even suggested his soloists play the same solo they had played on recordings. Most believed that was Miller's real success in the band business.

Benny, some of his sidemen said, had more trouble finding a good danceable beat. He worked on finding the appropriate rhythm but it didn't appear to come naturally, a few believed.

Some thought that Benny's problem was not being able to read the music and keep the beat at the same time. It wasn't a problem for Ray Anthony who spent time with the Miller band and learned from the master nor was it a reach for Ralph Flanagan who spent years with a number of veteran big bands before he stood in front of his own. His orchestra had that built in beat that fit the bunny hop generation and gave dancers a gliding music also similar to Miller.

Big band musicians and leaders spent every hour of every day crafting music and sounds that would give them gigs, recording dates and ways to make the money they weren't making. Radio, which had increased the popularity of dance music throughout the country, was free and while it produced fans, it didn't produce an income flow leaders reported. Fans looked forward to weekend big band dates from all the exciting spots in the country without leaving their homes. "I was a veteran big band listener," said the late Utica (NY) Observer-Dispatch editor and columnist Harold Whittemore. "I scheduled my evenings to hear the bands. Give me 15 seconds of music and I could name the band—that is, if they played in the mid-1930s and early 1940s. They'd be what people called Mickey Mouse or tick-tock bands but I loved their music. I'm talking about Emery Deutsch, Russ Morgan, Freddy Martin, Henry King, Eddie Duchin, Jan Garber, Johnny Long, Shep Fields, Sammy Kaye, Miller and, of course, Lawrence Welk from the Aragon and Trianon in Chicago along with Hal Kemp and Guy Lombardo. We used to catch all these bands on remote broadcasts late at night. I really liked Ace Brogode and his Virginians. Never heard the band or him again through 40 years of writing columns but I did do one column about him. I actually heard from one reader who remembered him, too." [1]

The society band was so named because it offered a type of soft, distinguishable non-jazz but pleasant music that aristocratic people sought when they went for an evening of dancing and socializing. Remember jazz musicians already had a reputation for playing bars and taverns where unsavory behavior was the norm. Blaring loud music wasn't acceptable in reputable restaurants, hotel ballrooms and clubs of the 1930s. Their well coiffed and manicured guests wouldn't tolerated it, they felt. Don't forget the scenes in the *Gene Krupa Story* where owners were outraged at bands that played jazz or misrepresented themselves. Today we have grocery store and automated-sounding mall music. In the 20s and 30s radio filled the air with soothing classical and soft sounds… in the 1930s to 1950s there was country club music which featured muted brass, blended saxophones, piano, bass and drums played with wire brushes to lessen the "noise" level of the instrument. Its purpose clearly was to offer background entertainment to your table conversations and yet be ready for you when you decided to dance. It was Legato music with a softness that gave dancers and listeners an uplifting feeling.

Hotel, ballroom and even club owners were zealously protective of their audiences, too. I once played a hotel on a holiday night in northern Ohio where our piano player had spent weeks arranging a Christmas medley of carols and traditional holiday music for the evening's dancing. We started with the medley in the second set and within minutes the owner came to the leader very angry. Our leader ended the medley quickly and we segued into *Frosty the Snowman* I think. At the break, we discovered the owner was agitated that we were playing sacred music—Christmas carols like *Hark the Herald Angels Sing*—that should NOT be played for dancing! One of those unspoken and not written down rules of the business.

The bandleaders of such musical groups were a particular type of debonair, fashionable and smooth talking performer. But not all were successful. A child prodigy on the trombone with a romantic tone and quality built for success, bandleader Bobby Byrne of Columbus, OH, was considered to be headed for stardom within months of organizing his group. People called him "brilliant" and "amazing" and were waiting for his rise on Billboard's list. His band was capable, critics said, but Bobby's frustration over perfection got in the way. Some said he tried too hard. His big break came in 1941 when Frank Dailey scored an entertainment coup by booking the Byrne band at the Meadowbrook just ahead of its appearance at the Glen Island Casino, two of the top east coast dance spots. Regular radio remotes and a record contract with Decca put him on a fast track. Personnel problems hampered him when his singer Dorothy Claire left and then he suffered a severe appendicitis while he was playing an engagement at New York City's Strand Theater. Other bandleaders demonstrated how much his friends thought of him and his music when they voluntarily fronted his band during their free time while he convalesced.

But the events caused him the kind of irritation you have to avoid. A tense and very dedicated person, he ignored the typical advice to slow down.

He worked his band seven days a week adding rehearsals to a busy schedule. He wouldn't tolerate wrong notes called "clams" and he was determined to integrate new but complicated arrangements from talented Don Redman. It didn't work. He started to hit the right notes later but by late 1942 he disbanded and accepted a commission in the Army Air Corps that had offered Glenn Miller his mili-

> *Nothing in life is more important than serving good music to 'society.'*

tary career. After the war he formed another orchestra but he folded it after a few years. Said many of his friends and musical compatriots, he was a gifted musician but his timing wasn't good. It was the nature of the business as witnessed by Miller who had started and folded his first band a few years earlier.

Time Magazine summed up the stereotype in a 1959 summer article called

Society Band. "In the yacht and country clubs and the looming shingled mansions by the sea, eastern high society dances the summer nights away to the honey-tongued music of a few favored bands. The men on the band-stands at Newport, Southampton and Bar Harbor are the same ones who whip out the frothy fox trots at the coming-out balls in the fall, at the cano-pied weddings in June; two generations of debutantes have been presented, courted and married under the batons of such bandleaders as Meyer Davis and Emil Coleman. Perhaps the busiest of the musical blue books is a springy, raw-nerved little man named Lester Lanin, who believes that nothing in life is more important than serving good music to 'society.'"

The magazine's description is exactly what any society page reader of the era conjured when he thought about an upcoming country club dance. *Time* knew its audience, too.

While the elite knew and got exactly what they wanted from their club or favorite night club, out in middle America young people and their par-ents tried to capture what the rich were doing. Consequently, bands led by people like Vincent Lopez, Kay Kyser, Larry Clinton, Vaughn Monroe, Ozzie Nelson, Horace Heidt, Doc Peyton, Jan Campbell, Fred Waring, Wayne King, Carmen Cavallero, Buddy Rogers, Ted Fio Rito, Abe Lyman, Alvino Rey, Orrin Tucker, Tommy Tucker, Lee Castle, Henry Busse, Russ Morgan, Paul Whiteman, Eddy Howard, Dick Jurgens, Guy Lombardo, Jan Garber, Ben Selvin, Ernie Hecksher, Anson Weeks, Ted Straeter, Gray Gordon, Shep Fields, Lawrence Welk, Blue Barron, Frankie Carle, Freddie Martin, Johnny Long, Eliot Lawrence, Ben Bernie, Sammy Kaye and novelty bandleader Ted Lewis met the strict guidelines applied to bands that got the gigs. Some of the unwritten rules included:

If playing an Elks Lodge, music can be stopped (mid-chorus sometimes) at 11 p.m. for a ritual all Elk Club members participated in.

Dance sets were carefully arranged with an informal 80/20 rule; gentle two/four tempos 80 percent of the set and several two beat or bright Dixie numbers to either end the set or strategically placed near the end.

All requests within reason were honored if the leader had it in the music he carried. Some leaders talked about carrying 150 arrangements for such dances to impress the patrons they could play anything.

If playing for a very old crowd or ethnic gathering you could expect calls for waltzes, polkas or German drinking songs and while even society bands were hard-pressed to carry such sheet music, some bandleaders were adept by having older members or a piano player who could play the melo-dies and help the audience sing along or dance to old favorites. They always turned out to be crowd pleasers. I played with several territory bands where a number of sets were devoted to such requests and we knew we delighted audiences because of the applause and appreciative comments that came unsolicited when we finished. They heard "their music," thanks to our band. Yet as young modern musicians, we balked at playing music "beneath" our lofty standards; for example, country music.

Local bands could gain a terrific advantage over name groups or others if they knew or prepared themselves by having the music of the local public high school or college school songs. It was that personal touch that made the performance memorable to the crowd which left happy although the band usually felt the evening was hardly "artistically satisfying." It meant doing your homework to play a gig.

Kaye, a native Ohioan, who was born Samuel Zarnocray Jr. in Rocky River, created his own success shortly after graduating from Ohio University in 1928 in civil engineering, by realizing his degree wouldn't help him in an economic depression and he decided to pursue his musical interest as a clarinetist and saxophonist. His "sweet" band success at OU and throughout the state continued as the "Swing and Sway" Sammy Kaye Orchestra which featured a Glee Club. A song writer, Kaye collaborated with Don Reid and wrote a World War II ditty called *Remember Pearl Harbor* which gave the band more notoriety.

The Kaye band could take dancers, listeners and lovers down a wonderful memory lane of melody hits. The classics were *Daddy, It Isn't Fair* and *Harbor Lights*. Another favorite portion of the repertoire was a feature called *So You Want to Lead a Band* which gave audience members a chance to lead the orchestra. The Kaye band continues today directed by college professor and former trumpet player, Roger Thorpe.

Guy Lombardo, said Lou DiSario, who introduced him to audiences over the years at Atlantic City's fabled Steel Pier and Hamid Ballrooms, was the friendliest bandleader of the hundreds of touring musicians he worked with. "He made you feel important in a business of far too many self-important people. You could talk to him about anything and get an intelligent response unlike others like Goodman or Miller. Too often, you got a distant look or a shrug from other name personalities."

Lou recalled how he passed up a chance

Ted Lewis   Photo courtesy of Behren's Family Archive

of a lifetime at the old Hamid Ballroom where he managed the dance hall and even taught dancing. "Guy knew I was a singer and dancer with professional experience and he frequently asked me what numbers to play for particular crowds at the ballroom… and he would take my advice, too. I remember that fans during the post-war years—1946 I think— really loved his versions of *It's Love, It's Love* and *Speak Low*. One time, his manager came over to me and asked me to join the Lombardo Orchestra on tour. Go on the road with the top sweet band in the country! It was a terrific opportunity! But I couldn't. I couldn't give up a secure position with the City of Philadelphia and lose out on a good pension. I had a family and obligations. You kick yourself later over and over but you know you made the right call for the family," Lou said wistfully. You rarely got a second chance I discovered.

Lombardo was somewhere between a society and simply a sweet band, Lou told me. "The society band took on a look of culture to fit the crowd and that meant acting more aloof. Nothing demeaning certainly but the look was different than your average band. Sweet bands were more ordinary guys with good dispositions and good at reading charts and offering what the leader and the audiences wanted." [2]

Lombardo later told Christopher Popa (www.BigBandLibrary.com) his recipe for success started and ended with the audience. "The aspiring bandleader will soon learn that the quickest way to incur the public's displeasure is to ignore its requests for songs… 80 percent of success will depend on ability to play the songs the public wants to hear. The remaining 20 percent will depend on his style, personality, the breaks and various other factors. As soon as I see that no one is getting up to dance or that there is a buzz of conversation around the room, I know they aren't listening and aren't even interested in what's being played. This is my cue to take the song out of my book."

The competition was always keen enough that band leaders felt compelled to seek different sounds and images to promote themselves. Local bands probably faced more competition for fewer venues than did touring groups. Dick Trimble, a Central Ohio orchestra, bought a half hour block of time on the local radio station to showcase the danceable music his band played. Others did the same. And timing was important. He bought his time in early fall recognizing that

Charlie Spivak   Photo courtesy of James Ronan Collection, IA

fall, at that time, was more important for winter dances than spring. He included spring in later years.

A significant number of high school musicians in the 1940s and '50s remember their days in area society orchestras. Good friend, Al Nerino of Bangor, PA, has such reminisces of days and the gigs. He began learning the fundamentals of trombone in high school with a maestro from an Italian conservatory who had moved to the Italian-American community of Roseto, PA. "But I wanted to get lessons from more modern guys so I started with trombonist Fred Miller from my hometown who played with bandleaders Charlie Spivak and Johnny Long among others. His tips helped me move from amateur to fair to middling trombonist. He taught me how to use my lip instead of my tongue in moving from note to note," Al continues. "I got my chance to play professionally when I was recruited from among the best instrumentalists in the high school band to join the DeMarco Dance Band." The DeMarco Band carried three trumpets, two trombones, three reeds, a bass, guitarist, a pianist and a drummer. "We used stock arrangements and played Knights of Columbus, Masons, Kiwanis, Elks and church affairs in the area. We weren't union so our pay was determined by the leader who decided what he thought was fair," Al says. The young trombonist continued to learn more about his instrument from DeMarco. "He taught me how to change G-clef music to Bass (F) clef by just adding three flats to the key signature. If the key was A Major each flat canceled a sharp designated in the signature key so that I would play it in the key of C. If the key was D Major each sharp would be canceled and one flat would be left so the key then would be F Major. It sounds complicated but really it wasn't and more important, it worked."

Al went on to Penn State where he answered an ad in the student newspaper and joined a newly formed college band. "When I arrived at the first practice, there was one other trombone player and he didn't want to be first chair so I inherited the spot the first practice. We had two trumpets, two trombones, two reeds, a piano player who was also the leader and a drummer. Our leader, a music major, got stock arrangements and scheduled our gigs. The band used his name which I can't remember first and then later we became the Musical Knights. We played fraternity dances on Saturday nights and during my two years with the group, we played some dances for community organizations. We weren't union but we still got jobs and the union groups must not have complained. There must have been a lot of opportunities because no one called us on our appearances. The leader must have had a relative working for some music publisher because he would come up with one or two arrangements every week. We had some good musicians who were very good at sight reading," he continued.

What were the perks of playing in a college-based band in central Pennsylvania during the 1950s?

"One was playing for fraternities and being invited to have supper before the dances started. We would get there early and eat in the kitchen. All the cooks were excellent and the food was delicious. If we had a new arrangement to go over we would do it before the dance started," he said.

But staffing was as difficult for territory bands as it was for touring bands. "Saturday nights became problem times for leaders. One or two of our group would either go home or have something important to do and couldn't play and if the leader couldn't get a replacement we would play shorthanded. One week, for example, two trumpet players couldn't make it and without the trumpet section we thought we would have to tell the fraternity president we couldn't make it," Al remembered. But Al was willing to take a gamble. He told the leader he thought he could handle the trumpet parts by using the conversion trick with the three flats he had learned earlier.

"We played the gig and I added the three flats and played an octave higher for most of the songs. There wasn't anything too tricky with any of our arrangements and the leader was satisfied. No one at the Saturday dance noticed anything different," he laughed. His double duty paid dividends. "I got paid double that night for using my trombone to handle trumpet parts," he noted. "Funny thing I never had to do it again on the job but today when I get a music book in G-clef I like to play tunes on my trombone."

Al played his sophomore and junior years but studying, doing a journalism internship for the local paper "made continuing a struggle even though we didn't play every weekend. Finally, I felt it was time to leave the band." [3]

Typically, for those who enjoyed the music and had talent many pursued other careers for very practical reasons. Fred Kircher of Burlington, NC, remembers growing up in the backyard of New York City, big bands and night spots. "I grew up in Bloomfield, NJ which was within train and bus distance to the theatres in New York City and Newark, NJ where the travel bands played in the late 1930s and early '40s. Bloomfield was close to Frank Dailey's Meadowbrook Ballroom in Cedar Grove. I was in the right place at the right time to see and hear most of the big travel bands," he recalls.

"I started playing trombone in grammar school and the man who lived next door played in Frank Dailey's Orchestra before he took over the ballroom. He would give me some trombone lessons when he was home which wasn't often. But I decided that if I wanted a normal home life it would not be as a musician. Music is a great source of pleasure but it wasn't going to be a business for me. I did play trombone for approximately 45 years in community symphonic orchestras, concert bands, semi-professional musical theatre and even with a Dixieland group. I loved music but I didn't see it as an income source. I never joined a union but I made it a personal policy out of respect to never play where I might put a union musician out of work," Fred said.

Touring bands frequently set the tone for society and sweet bands to capitalize on the proliferation of gentle and melodic sounds from a good number of song writers and arrangers. The public listened to the radio and late night remotes were popular from exciting ballrooms that many Americans never got the chance to see. But listening to the popular music of the day played by the Miller, Tommy Dorsey, Paul Whiteman or Benny Goodman bands made the songs familiar to people going to dances in their hometowns. And hometowners sometimes got a chance to show their talent with touring national bands. Betty Evans of Whitesboro, NY, wrote to her hometown newspaper in Utica, NY to describe how exciting her performance with the Shep Fields' band was. It was an amateur night at the Stanley Theater locally and she was thrilled to win the first night's competition at 14. She came in second in the final night.

Carole Crimmons of Frankfort told the Utica newspaper she still remembers several nights in 1949 when she was a guest soloist with the celebrated Harry James Orchestra. "I was 9 years old at the time and I felt like Cinderella at the ball," she told readers.

The Miller band, certainly, from 1939 to 1942 when he enlisted in the Army Air Corps created interest from hundreds of other bandleaders to get the charts of the numbers being played on the radio and in record stores. Glen's *Moonlight Serenade*, his theme, was quite popular but was second to Judy Garland's *Over the Rainbow* another big hit in 1939. However, Miller's productivity in recording studios with hit songs was a strong reason for his phenomenal rise in popularity. Besides *Moonlight Serenade* he had other hits such as *Man With the Mandolin, Moon Love, Stairway to the Stars*, and *Sunrise Serenade* the same year. A year later, he produced 10 more; *In The Mood, A Nightingale Song, In Berkeley Square, Careless, Fools Rush In, Imagination, It's A Blue World, Tuxedo Junction, When You Wish Upon A Star* and the *Woodpecker's Song*.

Miller insisted his band was a dance band that played swing and while some critics claimed he was far too commercial, his description was probably the best you could find. He didn't consider his band a "society" band but it could easily play such arrangements and handle such engagements.

Three years before his death in 1944, he recorded 12 other hits and near-hits and he continued recording on the V-Disc program for military service audiences serving overseas. They weren't released for commercial purposes and demonstrated once more his patriotism and service to his country.

Territorial bands like that of Manny Green of Galveston, TX, helped make music a part of social life in Texas. Manny started his band in 1948 three years after spending 36 months battling the Japanese on Guadalcanal and the Philippines. Said his longtime friend and former band singer, Frankie Catoe, at his death in 2007: "To all the dancers, he was what music should be. He had a gift and he knew what would pick those feet up." According Kevin Moran of the *Houston Chronicle*, Houstonians filled ballrooms at the city's swank Shamrock and Rice hotels to dance to Green's original arrangements of popular big band music. Manny collaborated with Lew Quadling, a Hollywood arranger and composer for Lawrence Welk on the television show. At his death in 2007, Manny had 700 arrangements for his 12-piece band. His band played the National Republican Convention in Houston in 1992 among many gigs in the southwest. He played dances at night and handled shifts as a captain in the warrant and criminal bailiffs division of the Galveston County Sheriff's Department for 22 years.

Society bands gained even more popularity among the early radio audience because of the glamorous places they played and the music they used for their broadcasts. *Wikipedia* offers an interesting account of the big band remotes in the 1930s and '40s and the appeal of these broadcasts. Said the non-profit web site:

"As early as 1923 listeners could tune in The Waldorf-Astoria Orchestra. The Oriole Orchestra (Dan Russo and Ted FioRito) was performing at Chicago's Edgewater Beach Hotel when they did their first radio remote broadcast on March 29, 1924, and two years later, they opened the famous Aragon Ballroom in July 1926, doing radio remotes nationally from the Aragon and the Trianon Ballrooms. In 1929, after Rudy Vallee's Orchestra vacated Manhattan's Heigh-Ho Club to do a movie in Hollywood, Will Osborne's dance band found fame with a nationwide audience

Eddie Howard　Photo courtesy of Lou DiSario

due to radio remotes from the Heigh-Ho. By 1930, Ben Bernie was heard in weekly remotes from Manhattan's Roosevelt Hotel.

"Broadcasts were usually transmitted by the major radio networks directly from hotels, ballrooms, restaurants and clubs. During World War II, the remote locations expanded to include military bases and defense plants. Band remotes mostly originated in major cities, including Boston, Los Angeles, New York, Philadelpha, San Francisco and Chicago. The Chicago broadcasts featured bands headed by Count Basie, Frankie Carle, Duke Ellington, Jan Garber, Jerry Gray, Woody Herman, Earl Hines, Eddie Howard (from the Aragon Ballroom), Dick Jurgens, Kay Kyser (from the Blackhawk Restaurant), Coon-Sanders Original NightHawk Orchestra (from the Blackhawk), Ted Weems, Shep Fields (from the Palmer House) and Griff Williams. The usual procedure involved the network sending a two-man team, announcer and engineer, with remote radio equipment to a designated location. The announcer would open with music behind an introduction "Coming to you from Frank Dailey's Meadowbrook on Route 23, just off the Pompton Turnpike in Cedar Grove, New Jersey, we present the music of Charlie Barnet and his Orchestra" or from a few miles away "For your dancing pleasure Columbia brings you the music of Count Basie and his Orchestra, coming to you from the Famous Door on Fifty-Second Street in New York City…" [4]

To a youngster like me and thousands of other Midwesterners there was the excitement of hearing themes which we all knew by note, melody and tempo. We couldn't tape it—such equipment wasn't available in the late 1930s and early '40s— and you prayed there wouldn't be static somewhere on the eastern seaboard or off Lake Erie around Cleveland! You usually had to have permission to stay up beyond 11 p.m. (which was the time for many of the late night big band remotes) and you thoroughly absorbed every minute and put them to memory. If you had the 78 recording, you played it the next day to make sure the band or the soloist played it as you remembered it. Usually they did.

The music of most society bands was similar. Some bandleaders, most the touring bands for example, maintained their distinctiveness with arrangers who gave each number their signature and style. Bands like Lombardo, Fields, Lanin and others needed separation from the field to ensure their identity and considering the number of years they prospered, they were most successful. Yet, on the way to well-earned recognition came humbling experiences, too. Sometimes embarrassing episodes you had to swallow.

Horace Heidt, for example, a legendary bandleader and radio and TV personality who started a number of talented people to success, was a decent piano player who used to tell audiences he became a musician because of a college football injury. He got his start playing at California's Claremont Hotel. The featured attraction with him on that early billing was a trained German shepherd named "Lobo."

"I was leery of any billing that included somebody named 'Lobo' after that," he laughed. During his years of finding talent he brought us musicians and singers such as pianist Frankie Carle, guitarist Alvino Rey, bandleader Warren Covington, trumpeter Bobby Hackett, singer Gordon MacRae and then singer and later comedian, Art Carney.

Territorial bands, by contrast, needed versatility considering the limits of their geography.

High society meant special types of dances, frequently called balls. They continue in virtually every part of America today and have evolved from private affairs to public events that sponsor everything from the humane society to United Nations activities. They are formal attire affairs and for musicians that means buying or renting a tuxedo. At times it was another stressful situation for leaders and musicians of territorial bands where it was another cost. In the 1930s through the 1950s you used any suit that was dark blue or black to make do. Nothing like playing a gig for less than $50 and having to buy a tux or even rent one that took half the income or more. They also required music appropriate to the events and a leader with the personality to deal with dignitaries either on the national scene or local. As any bandleader will tell you vanity is huge and massaging such egos takes a great deal of humility.

Lester Lanin was one of the best most believe. By his count, he played for 20,000 weddings and bar mitzvahs, debutante balls, celebrity galas and offered music for such world renown as Prince Charles and Diana, Queen Elizabeth II who actually changed her 60th birthday party to fit into Lanin's schedule and the inaugural balls of every president from Dwight Eisenhower to Bill Clinton. Jimmy Carter and George W. Bush didn't use Lanin's music.

And you paid to have Lanin music. His fee could be in the range of $75,000 for a single night. His work kept him extremely busy. He never took a vacation and he worked every year until his death in 2004 at 97. He wasn't a music innovator but he certainly knew how to please his hosts and their parties. Lester's dapper attitude and discretion were a perfect fit for the high society crowd. He told those who wanted to use his orchestra that the band could play most songs written after 1920 and it also handled light classics, polkas, popular rock-'n-roll and Irish lullabyes. His goal he said time and time again was "to keep people moving on the dance floor, smiling and having a good time." Said one Englishwoman, a Lanin fan, "That marvelous Lester would have made an earthworm want to dance!"

A Lanin event might evolve the way Karim Aga Khan's party to celebrate the birth of his daughter Princess Zahra in 1988. An exclusive party for 800 guests at their chateau near Paris featured special food flown in from America; caviar, smoked salmon and vintage champagne. The fireworks after the dinner were reported to have cost $300,000. That's not considered a problem for the 100 richest men and women in America and the kings of Norway, Spain, Greece, Denmark and Sweden who have used his musical services over the years.

Said *USA Today* in reviewing Lanin's years in 1992: "For generations of the rich and famous, a society party isn't a society party unless Lanin is there with his back to the tuxedoed crowd." The memories of a Lanin event still permeate eastern society.

Finding particular musicians who were talented and discreet wasn't easy from the 1930s through 2004. Most union members weren't church organists and ensuring that the music would be smooth, contemporary and danceable kept the leader busy especially maintaining quality when you've got more than 1,500 musicians working every weekend. Like a few other bandleaders, affable Lester wouldn't tolerate drinking, drug use or smoking on the bandstand. Not an easy policy to enforce in the 1960s and '70s.

While he tried to remain contemporary, his critics complained about the monotony of his rhythms and the seamless sameness of his music; endless numbers run together in long medleys.

Said a review on Spaceagepop.com: "He's probably fused twist, bossa nova, soul, disco, funk, punk, hip-hop and rap into his medleys at sometime or other—unfortunately for us, never all at once." Such sameness can be wearisome too. One savvy musician remembered a wedding the band played where the groom asked Lanin to play "Take Five" the famous Dave Brubeck five quintuple time innovative number. Lester didn't hesitate. He called it up thinking the band had the arrangement. He bravely tried to conduct this 5/4 time number and tried to get the drummer's help to set some kind of tempo within the medley only to give up after several choruses and yelled for the band to transition to "Five Foot Two with Eyes of Blue." But he segued without losing his cool, bystanders said.

Are society balls a thing of the past? Not really. Local non-profits, fraternal organizations, civic groups, museums, political affairs, high school and college events are just as popular today as they were in the 18th century.

Yet it becomes more difficult each year to replace orchestras from that early era like Wayne King who were polished personalities, modest in presentation yet ideal at making an event a memorable one.

King, for example, was a professional football player with the Canton (OH) Bulldogs before he made music his career demonstrating that you could come from almost any background to join the genteel world of the upper class and entertain socialites. He started on the saxophone in the Whiteman orchestra before he organized the Wayne King Orchestra in 1927. Like other bandleaders he disbanded at the outbreak of World War II and joined the army where he was promoted to major before leaving in 1946. Three years later, Wayne had his own television show and was honored with a star on the Hollywood Walk in the radio category. Later in life, he operated a Black Angus cattle farm and a car rental business. Who said there isn't a career path to and from music?

A national social affair that takes place every four years in Washington, DC is the tradition of presidential balls. President Obama's Inaugural held 26 balls at everywhere from the Smithsonian to the Washington Hilton. They represented, as they usually do, all walks of life and the president is expected to pop in at each during the course of the evening and early morning.

The 2009 balls included the All American Ball, American Scholars Ball, Black Tie and Boots Ball, Change Has Come Inaugural Ball, Commander in Chief Ball, one of three official balls; Hey, America Feels Cool Again Inaugural Ball and a number of state functions. More than 1,400 celebrated the North Carolina Society Ball at the Marriott Wardman Park Hotel near the National Zoo. The band? Certainly wasn't Lester's orchestra… it was Chapel Hill's Liquid Pleasure which played Motown, soul and funk music while guests ate grits and drank martinis.

> *Neal and his orchestra were "as much a part of the social season as black tie and champagne"*

Said bandleader Kenny Mann about keeping people on the floor during the evening: "There's nothing more fun than having a bunch of old people dancing to Snoop Doggy Dogg at midnight."

We've lost a number of celebrity bandleaders from the early days. Names like Lombardo, Lanin, Eddie Howard, Duchin and Carmen Cavallero are gone although they resurface from time to time when a veteran from the band gets a gig to play. And we're also losing territorial leaders who were veritable institutions in their regions of the country. Neal Smith of Florida was an example. Said Shannon Donnelly of the *Palm Beach Daily News*, FL: Neal and his orchestra were "as much a part of the social season as black tie and champagne" when he died at 91 in 2008.

Smith was a medic during World War II and when he returned to West Palm Beach, he picked up his e-flat clarinet and started playing with his band, The Three Bad Habits. He played at Werts where he met Freddie Frink, who became Mrs. Smith. He was a man who smiled easily and a person of great loyalty. He and his wife were a team at Palm Beach events until her death in 2000. In the 1960s, he and co-leader pianist Cliff Hall introduced their big band. Neal continued Hall's share of the enterprise when the pianist became ill and unable to play. He eventually died. The Smith-Hall orchestra played debutante parties, weddings, and charity balls and their popularity took them far beyond Florida shores. The orchestra played exclusive black tie affairs in Rome, Athens, Sidney, Hong Kong and Madrid.

The affable bandleader also did such premier events as President George Bush's 1989 inaugural ball, 24 consecutive Flamingo Balls, 30 of Maryland socialite Marylou Whitney's Derby parties in Kentucky and 28 consecutive International Red Cross Balls in Palm Beach. He played the Coconut every New Year's Eve and the opening party at the Everglades Club each year, too. Said Guy Scott, the orchestra's pianist since 1973:

"Neal was the classic Southern gentleman. I remember we were in Chicago to play for the 100th anniversary celebration of the Chicago Symphony. We checked into the Congress Hotel at 2 a.m. and there was an elderly woman scrubbing the floor. He said to me: 'A woman her age shouldn't be doing that kind of work' and he went over to her and told her how much he respected her work ethic. He reaches into his pocket and pulled out a lot of money and pressed it into her hand. She cried. That's the kind of man he was."

And society orchestras continue to thrive during good times and bad as communities celebrate their civic events and take time to enjoy themselves for good causes. And most observers believe they will continue.

You could be watching future national political leaders when you saw a number of society bands in the 1940s. Bandleader Henry Jerome employed two sidemen who would leave for more famous positions. In the reed section was future chairman of the Federal Reserve Alan Greenspan on bass clarinet and sitting beside him was President Richard Nixon's White House Counsel Leonard Garment on saxophone. The story is that both men met while playing for Henry and Garment recommended Alan to become Nixon's chairman of the Council of Economic Advisers before his selection to the Federal Reserve Board.

In Central Iowa, the High Society Big Band, a 16 piece black tie organization, takes you back to those days with a delightful panorama of historic swing era of the 1930s, '40s and '50s and the sounds of Goodman, James, Kenton, Ellington, the Dorseys, Miller and Count Basie among others. The orchestra plays annual events like the Red Friars Dance Club in Ames and it has been the evening's entertainment at the Mary Greeley Medical Center Auxiliary dinner and auction and the Habitat for Humanity Grand Gala Ball.

Society events, it seems, are delightful places to dance to soft, melodic music.

1. Letter from Harold Whittemore, Aug. 22, 1989
2. Letter from Lou DiSario, Feb. 27, 2002
3. Letter from Al Nerino, Dec. 22, 2004
4. en.Wikipedia.org/wiki/Big_band-remotes

Many Think The Beat

Made Big Bands Popular

No one has a definitive answer to the popularity of the big band era and dance bands of the 1930s and later. Certainly the music and the orchestrations by black and white arrangers had something to do with it. The need to socialize (dance) was a part too. But a more powerful element may have been the beat and the leader's ability to set a tempo that enticed people onto the dance floor.

One of the strengths of the Glenn Miller band which took the country by storm in the late 1930s and continued into the 1940s was Glenn's ability to set a tempo that old and young could tap their feet to and clap their hands in rhythm. Though Glenn, a modest and shy man, was never known to encourage listeners—even dancers—to do anything, the music and beat created a natural urge to respond.

Did the beat make big bands, dance music popular?

Michael Berkowitz, licensed leader of the Gene Krupa Orchestra, thinks it's an interesting premise. "Certainly since the beginning of time people have been beating out rhythms on hollowed logs, pots, rocks and drums. All life has rhythm…tempo, beginnings, endings. So, did the beat attract people to the big bands? Perhaps."

A creative way to reinforce dance music's popularity locally was the use of a local radio station. Dick Trimble, a bandleader in Lancaster, OH was an astute businessman who recognized that his band's music needed to be heard as often as possible especially during the months when social events were planned.

Dick followed Glenn Miller's public relations plan which was to let his music sell the band's appeal. Listeners to Sunday afternoon radio heard "Tempos with the Trimble Treatment" which offered a mixture of Dixie, ballads by vocalists and current Hit Parade numbers. There was little talk by announcer Dick Westbrook which allowed many songs to be played in the time slot. Hits with an uptempo beat such as *I've Got My Love to Keep Me Warm*, Dixie numbers such as *Sister Kate* and fun numbers like *Come on to My House* were coupled with slow ballads such as *Blue Velvet, Moonlight in Vermont* and special arrangements of medleys of George Shearing hits done by high school teacher and trombonist Bob Bechtel offered the band's repertoire and demonstrated the illusion of dancing away the coming weekends during dreary winter months.

It was a band that wanted to please dancers and listeners and did just that. The beat, of course, was always present in the music. The Trimble band had a lengthy stay at a downtown armory doing Friday night YMCA dances for young people and at a local country club handling holiday dances.

Dick Trimble Band   Photo courtesy of Chuz Alfred

A Trimble fan from the 1950s said what many felt: "I loved to go to the lake on a warm weekend evening with whoever I was going with at the time, walk up the wooden steps to the ballroom, find a booth usually filled with friends and wait for the music. What a thrill, dancing to music in an open pavilion. Besides a Coke, you couldn't ask for more." Another attended Y dances and his memories linger to this day. "The place was cavernous, the sound wasn't good and the building looked like it hadn't been cleaned inside or out for centuries but it came alive for me every Friday night with the Dick Trimble band. You looked forward to dancing and enjoying a good band playing the hits every weekend." It was the memory many seniors still retain decades later.

What is a good tempo? In a web discussion, musicians and others debated the issue. Drummers are always prejudiced about the subject but even brass and woodwind players feel the beat is a way to excite a crowd of people whether to dance, sway back and forth or tap their toes to the tempo.[1]

Is there a good beat for songs? Said one web wag: "It really isn't quantifiable in bpm (beats per minute). A good analogy is trying to gauge how warm the weather is. If its been cold for a while and you get one sunny day, you'll say warm. But if you're in the middle of a heat wave and you get one cloudy day, you'll be glad of how cool it is. And if you ask an African and then an Inuit… well, you get the idea. The important thing though is that you are comfortable with your speed and you are playing all the notes (including rolls, etc). If you are having any doubts, simply take it down a notch."

How does that translate? Woody Herman probably wouldn't take it down a beat and neither would Stan Kenton. Guy Lombardo, Sammy Kaye, Vincent Lopez and others would drop the beat out of respect for the dancers more than likely.

Lester Lanin, who probably would have surprised everyone by keeping the beat as it was but converting it to two beat, did more to popularize society dancing than any leader in the 20th century especially with the east coast elite. He was the first to create a continuous stream of dance music with changes in tempo. He made popular what was called the "business man's bounce," an uptempo two-beat that fit in context with the stream of music in a set. Consequently, he kept dancers on the floor. He even innovated a way to move the tempo from Dixie to rock'n'roll. The purpose? Given the cost of his orchestra, it made those paying for such events believe they got their money's worth. And most agreed.

His success came year after year and by word of mouth among the comfortable who gave him little to worry about during the Depression. He told the *New York Times* in 1995 "You play one day and it's like a mustard seed—it grows. Someone says 'I heard you play at such and such a party, then someone else says it and before you know it, you're playing lots of parties.'"

Imagine operating a dance band during the Depression profitably! Lester did. Said the reliable web site nfo.net/usa, "Lester Lanin's orchestra would go on to ride out the Great Depression playing his eminently danceable music for the wealthiest families, both at home and abroad. The next 60 years were spent playing for such patrons as the British royal family and most of the kings and queens of Europe. In addition, beginning with the Eisenhower era, he played inaugural balls at the White House through nine presidencies."

His answer to the question about a danceable beat was as simple as his amazing success. He studied dancers on the floor, he said. "I watch their feet," he told the *Christian Science Monitor.* "If they're out of meter, something's wrong."

Other bandleaders interested in keeping their groups in demand pursued similar observations.

A complaint that bandleaders sometimes heard after playing a gig was that there were too many breaks, not enough music. Lester wouldn't let breaks be too long. He also refused to let his musicians drink or smoke on the bandstand. It could bring dismissal… although I found little evidence. You would experience more volatility from Buddy Rich, Benny Goodman and dozens of other nationally known bandleaders. They dismissed people on the spot.

Lanin was well aware of such complaints and he made sure that his band gave the wedding party plenty of dance music even though the interludes—the cutting of the cake, group pictures and a variety of other extra curricular events— were frequently caused by the party organizers. Lester was the consummate leader who made details his concern and the dance date the most important event of the moment. His popularity soared from the time he started in the late 1920s. He began as a piano player and then as a drummer at age 5. He thought he wanted to be a lawyer but changed direction when he dropped out of school at 15 and began recruiting musicians like Louie Armstrong, Jimmy and Tommy Dorsey as well as Doc Severinsen for his six brothers' bands. His father and grandfather were both bandleaders so he knew the business early in life.

Lester trailblazed a surefire approach in a field that frequently forgot who created any band's success. "Serve the public!," he told a *Times'* reporter. "Whoever you play for, try and make sure you were part and parcel of something happy, so if the woman whose party it was sees you on the street 15 years from now, she'll say 'Lester, you made my party!'" A story from a 1987 *Forbes* magazine about Lanin made him legendary in the music business. Lester was playing a debutante's ball when he was approached by the host, a wealthy patron, who told Lester he didn't want the night to end. He started pressing large wads of bills into Lanin's hands to keep the continuous music stream going.

And it did. But it abruptly stopped when the man collapsed on the dance floor. He died the next day.

A southern bandleader, Henry Mason, who has been leading musical organizations for more than 30 years, realizes as Lester did that a danceable beat and the melody are as important to dancers today as they were yesterday.

The founder of Atlanta's *Sentimental Journey Orchestra*, a traditional regional band with a national reputation, the orchestra is well recognized as an outstanding modern day territorial group. Says Henry: "SJO plays the Great American Songbook about as well as anyone. "Their engagements tell you their music has been enjoyed by various kinds of audiences. The SJO orchestra played for Ted Turner's 50th birthday bash, for example, President Jimmy Carter's Nobel Peace Prize celebration in Georgia and it was providing music for dancing when the 75th anniversary party was held for Atlanta's celebrated Fox Theater. Henry moved to North Carolina to be closer to family but he still wanted to remain active. He substituted on local bands and then decided that North Carolinians would probably enjoy the music that had made SJO so successful. He launched a band called *The Revelers*. Why the name? Says Henry:

" A revel is a large and boisterous special event. The *NC Revelers* are a big and boisterous special band for special events. "It also fulfills a promise he made to his late father-in-law. "I promised him a full band for his party if he made it to 100. Since he didn't quite make it (he died in his 80s), the band name serves as my salute to his outlook on life," he says in the band's web site.

Dance music means what it says, Henry told me in an email. You don't try to embellish what is straightforward and acceptable to the public, he told me. The band is popular on college campuses but also feels at home playing fundraising events.

In a web column, drummer Ted Kirby says that every dance tempo is usually quoted in bars per minute. [2] A waltz, one of the slowest, is 30 **BPM** the same as a slow foxtrot. A Viennese waltz, by contrast, is 50 to 60 **BPM** and is still faster than a jive piece that is 44 **BPM**.

What makes the tempo so critical to a band's success? In an internet article by keyboardist John Jackaman entitled "Playing For Dancing" he observes "First let us get one thing straight, you will never please all the dancers on the floor, they are the most critical of all audiences. The reason for this is quite simple: audience participation. When you play for dancing you invite your audience to share your music in a very intimate way. "

United Kingdom keyboardist Robert Davies who plays for dances throughout the UK echoes Jackaman. "There is a difference between ballroom, Latin and old time as compared to sequence dancing. Regarding sequence dancing, I agree with Ted's comments on tempos, although playing all over the country for dancing, as I do, tempos do vary. There's no hard and fast rule, some people prefer a brisk quickstep, some a slower foxtrot, you never can tell… I adjust the tempos slightly depending on the age and agility of the dancers. I have heard very few complaints, but you can never please all the people all the time. I just try to please most of the people most of the time." The happy medium always wins the majority of the people a majority of the time.

But drummers with major touring bands in earlier times were busy playing gigs and more concerned about their sound. Duke Ellington's drummer Stephen Little, who was with him in his final years, remembers when music changed and rock'n'roll became the influence. "I don't remember bang-

When you play for dancing, you invite your audience to share your music in a very intimate way.

ing drums with any big band the way that I had to after rock. Rock took up the level of all music. Even classical music. And it left its mark; percussionists in symphony orchestras now use bigger drums and cymbals to play the same music that they played in the 1940s and 50s. I can only say that any drummer who plays any rock at all hit drums harder than Shelly (Mann) ever dreamed of playing them with Kenton," Stephen explained.

How did Duke mentor his drummer? Stephen laughed and told me "Duke had no drum charts. You just sat there and played…by ear. Of course, it was daunting," he laughed. "Lot of Duke's compositions were long. I asked him once what records I should listen to so I could learn the music. He said that he didn't want me to listen to any of them. I don't want you sounding like Sonny Greer he said. Do your own thing. It was almost unheard of in the music business because everyone has preconceived ideas about drumming."[3]

Lou DiSario of Philadelphia who spent years on stage, singing and dancing and working as manager of the Million Dollar Pier ballroom along the east coast said that there was no question that the beat—the tempo— was vital to the band and the dancers. "You knew it was going to be a difficult evening if the drummer was hesitant and the leader was 'beat deaf' at setting the tempo for dance numbers. Yet, it could happen. It even happened among some big name bands from time to time. There were leaders who really had trouble setting the beat. Supposedly Benny Goodman had a difficulty. It was rumored that trumpeter Harry James, an ex circus drummer before his bandleading days, set the rhythm in the Goodman band. If you listen to the James band from 40s and beyond, it had solid beats," he said.

Harry James   Photo courtesy of James Ronan Collection, IA

Mike Berkowitz believes that Gene Krupa's talent helped move the drums out front. "His looks and style plus his drumming ability were like magnets to audiences during his career. 'Go Gene go' was the chant and Gene went…*Sing, Sing, Sing* is still heard every day in some form or other on the radio, TV shows, movies, jingles…it's inescapable. That primal tom tom beat goes right to your core. With the GK band (of which I've been the leader for six years) audiences still demand *Sing, Sing Sing*. That driving floor tom introduction makes everyone a bobbysoxer or jitterbug again."

To musicians looking at the chart in their music stand, the score told them what the tempo should be. There are stories about some bandleaders who didn't trust themselves and carried a metronome (a device that registered one tick per second) to set a beat. Some bands spent most of the night's playing in largo (slow and solemn) or Langhetto (60-66 bpm) which is a little faster. Adagio (66-76 bpm) moves the tempo up and allegro (120-168 bpm) is considered a lively beat. Musicians who played for the Buddy Rich and Woody Herman bands say that the difference between the leaders was that Woody would use the terms in rehearsal to let the band know that the tempo was faster. Buddy, said one sideman, "just started counting the beat on his sticks and we launched the sucker!"

The beat has changed drastically in recent years. Some drummers use what is called a drum machine and headphones. Most of the time it is used for studio work but with many touring bands you can see drummers with headsets. To the uninitiated, they aren't used to prevent deafness (although with rock groups from the 60s to the present that is a worry whether real or not), it gives the drummer a cadence to stay with when things get wild and the need to stay on course is necessary. It synchronizes their playing to an electronic metronome, a click track. In any recording, this permits easy digital editing. But it's not uncommon to see a drummer with a major rock group on his throne with a headset. What does it offer? Say drummers on the web site *Music Machinery* editing with the click-track are all measures of equal duration and can be moved without concern that the timing will be off.[4] The downside? To experienced listeners whether drummers or fans, songs recorded with the click-track can sound too sterile, lacking life and feeling. It's the tech side of drumming, rhythm and performing that brings arguments within the ranks.

Drums, which in the early 1930s became the featured instrument of the rhythm section of the dance band, took on more celebrity status when a Chicago-born drummer named Gene Krupa who used his personality and flair for showmanship made the move to New York City where he found gigs to prove his ability with the beat and offer creative solos within the breaks. He is credited with moving the drum set from the back of the band to the front. A pit gig in George Gershwin's Broadway play *Strike Up the Band*, with the Red Nichols band offered him the exposure needed to break into the New York market.

In a web Krupa celebration site Gene was credited for what I remembered about him.[5] "Krupa played 'tastefully' when appropriate and kicked it when he soloed. Overall, I would say he 'projected' well. As you know, he was a complete entertainer who enjoyed the flashy riffs and licks (as did Buddy Rich). The stuff movies are made of. He was also quite a rudimentary drummer. There was no rehearsal for him when we played together. He just walked out on stage, took a bow and sat down and played. No surprise there, I suppose. But I was scared to death," said John Petters.

That's the Krupa I met at Buckeye Lake in 1948. His band bus pulled onto the hot asphalt in a brilliant afternoon early summer after playing in New York the night before. He was headed west for a group of one niters and then the band would swing south. I was looking for a taller man but he was a dynamic guy of short stature with a friendly yet shy personality. I stammered out my first name and he took it from there asking me if the Pier Ballroom management sent me . "No," I said, "they said that I could come out and help if you needed me." Gene laughed retorting "Jack, we can use you!" The next thing I knew I had three drum cases and music stands for 16 men in front of me. The bus driver wanted to get unloaded… now. Gene wanted to know where the band would be staying. The Lake Breeze Hotel (which was attached across a walk way with the Pier Ballroom) was the closest I told him and he said "right, the same as last time I was here." I started taking the equipment to the ballroom and trumpeter Don Fagerquist came along side and wanted to know if there was a laundry/dry cleaner nearby. I told him I didn't know… but I would find out. Most of the guys wore the flair collar shirts popular then and everyone I saw wore the trademark zoot suit cut pants that tapered at the ankle. At the time I figured they hadn't had time to change after the last gig.

Krupa still hadn't left the parking lot when I returned to pick up more of the equipment which by now was a pile that was sizable. We didn't have luggage carts like those used at airports and railroad stations so I lugged another load and then a third and a fourth. Krupa came up on the third trip and thanked me. We talked and he offered to buy me a drink that night and he asked if I needed a pass to get in. I told him that the Pier management always let me in because I helped out. "You're a good man," he smiled. That night, I had my drink; an RC Cola sitting at the bar with Gene and several musicians.

He was what everybody said, a very kind and nice person. Just a few years later I owned a Krupa model Slingerland drum set thanks to a reluctant father and Trimble drummer Kenny Carpenter. I lugged those heavy pearl embossed drums throughout Ohio and neighboring states. Could have been why I had three hernias over the years. I remember Fagerquist as a sharp looking, crewcut trumpeter player who was 21 when I met him (I was 15) and part of the bop influence in the Krupa band. He had joined the band at 17. Sadly, he died of kidney failure at 47.

Mike Berkowitz   Photo courtesy of Mike Berkowitz

Unlike drummers like Rich, Louie Bellson and Jack Sperling whose technical skills and speed in later years were superior, Krupa pioneered the drums for kids like me who loved his flair, his basics and certainly his showmanship. Most drummers of that era, I thought, could have been jugglers and dancers. There was a kinship I discovered between Krupa and Lionel Hampton, for example. Watching the two of them you saw the admiration for what each did. Both of course, had worked together with Benny Goodman. You had to admire their manual dexterity in dealing with sticks and brushes and their footwork which could match an organist.

The beat was central to Krupa and it made the band successful on the dance circuit. Gene's personality was also important to the band's success and his personal achievements. Listen to Mike Berkowitz as he described meeting Gene:

"After the set, I was ushered back to the small dressing room. Gene was in his tux shirt and no jacket, relaxing. Here came the millionth kid drummer wanting to meet his hero. I began asking questions and Gene was kind enough to answer every one of them, dumb as they may have been. He had a great love of children, coaching Little League baseball teams in Yonkers, NY, counseling, mentoring. He was a true gentleman…and a gentle man."[6]

Rich was a solo drummer who let his speed and technique speak for him. Bellson and Sperling were excellent technicians who backed many good bands on the road in the 1940s and 50s. I spent time observing Sperling who was the driving force with the Les Brown Band of Renown when the Bob Hope USO tour came to Korea and I traveled with the entourage to write about the trip for the *Pacific Stars & Stripes*. His speed and dexterity were dazzling but they also told me that my future in the field wasn't bright.

Recognizing superior talent also causes one to recognize lack of personal ability. Disappointing, but the reality of life.

Yet, the prominence of these drummers didn't overshadow the baby spotlights that used to light up the bandstand when a young Gene took a solo on *Drum Boogie, Sing, Sing, Sing* and other hits. Much of Gene's solos, say some percussion people, came from long rolls which were punctuated by bass hits.

His flair led to cheering and clapping when he had merely done rudimentary drills as compared to Rich and others who demonstrated power, stamina and discipline with the set in later years.

Mike Berkowitz remembers that his first exposure to big bands came from his parents' LPs. He learned to play along with Moe Purtill, Glenn Miller's drummer.

"The Miller band was not a hard swinging group. Glenn didn't want that. He was a dance band and that great Miller sound of Willie Schwartz on lead clarinet —who later befriended me when I was a 23 year-old playing on the Nelson Riddle band—was something special. Still is. Strange as it might seem, my first exposure to Gene Krupa came from watching the *Dennis The Menace Show* with Jay North as Dennis. Dennis is seen marching down the street in the opening sequence while beating on a bass drum. Mr. Wilson, Dennis' cranky next door neighbor, looks out his window to see what all the racket is about. When he sees Dennis, he says 'Well, he's no Gene Krupa.' Having never heard the name, I asked my parents who that was and they told me Gene was a famous drummer. Not a spectacular intro to Mr. Krupa!"

Dancers were usually oblivious to such things, too. But they did know a solid beat, a good melody and a band that showed enthusiasm for what it attempted to do.

It took a leader or his designate who could set a good beat and a drummer who kept the beat constant to make a dance memorable. Your choice of a dancing partner could make it a 5-star evening.

But you didn't always have to go out to have a good time dancing. My parents talked to me about going to house parties in the 1930s when they would roll up the rug in the living or dining room and everybody would dance to music from a victorola that had to be wound up after each 78 record was played. Few people today would be excited about staying home on a Friday or Saturday night to "hear" a big band on the radio or phonograph. In an era when a home or condo has high definition and surround sound television that can take up a wall in a room imagine spending an evening listening and not seeing your entertainment!

But that's what young and old did when they lived in the 1930s, '40s and even in the 50s when distant glamorous ballrooms, dance halls or restaurants in major cultural centers like Boston, New York City, Chicago, San

Francisco, Miami and elsewhere were magnets to the ears. Your imagination did the rest.

Remember the times: in 1939, a gallon of gas was 10 cents, a new car was $700, a complete 10 piece bedroom suite was $79.85 and a new Emerson bedroom radio was $9.95. Beginning in 1920, radio became a reliable friend

In an era when a home or condo has high definition and surround sound television that can take up a wall in a room imagine spending an evening listening and not seeing your entertainment!

to the public but music, the public said, was why they listened. In 1939, the country's number one band was Glenn Miller and his theme, *Moonlight Serenade* was second only to Judy Garland's *Over the Rainbow*. Kate Smith's *God Bless America* was third.

A crusade in New York City in the 1930s against burlesque houses left empty buildings in the middle of the Depression but at the same time, jazz music was becoming swing especially after Duke Ellington let people know what they were listening to on the radio; *It Don't Mean a Thing If It Ain't Got That Swing*. The country, meantime, was hearing a number of black bands from remotes in the city. There were the Count Basie, Lionel Hampton, Fletcher Henderson and Chick Webb bands along with Duke and others like Cab Calloway, Fats Waller taking white dancers inside clubs and dance halls that formerly only catered to blacks. Two female singers rose to fame also. Ella Fitzgerald and Billie Holiday offered different styling and they were later joined by an ex-Cotton Club showgirl Lena Horne who began singing as well as dancing.

At radio stations around the country, broadcasters were trying to figure ways to handle the need for music, satisfy new copyright protection and keep audiences. Dave Dodrill of West Virginia remembers what it was like working for a small rural radio station where management was less interested in buying records and more interested in creating income. "At the station I worked as a disk jockey in the mid-1950s we received reel to reel audio tapes of musical programs produced by the military branches of service. They promoted military service and featured big bands and singers from the era. They arrived two tapes at a time in very sturdy brown boxes. The stations were supposed to return the tapes to producers but I think stations used them for their own purposes. On our station, the tapes were a significant addition to our programming since the owners wouldn't spend any money on records or other materials," he explained.

The bandleader enterpriser of the era was possibly Duke. He spread his version of big band music when he broadcasted from the very popular Cotton Club. His strength was the fact that he kept his band on the road and continued a steady payroll for his musicians from the 1920s through the '30s and beyond. "The huge popularity of Ellington and the other bands of the swing era might possibly not have come about without the invention of consumer radios. Radios afforded listeners away from major cities and venues the opportunity to hear music they might not otherwise have for the first time broadcast live," said Associated Content in a web site (www.associatedcontent.com)

Tenor saxophonist Chuz Alfred, who spent a good part of his younger years on the road with his own group and playing with the touring Ralph Martiere Band, remembers it with more nostalgia and noted the transition. "So many have already moved on; guys with the band…Others I've known like Zoot, Cannonball, Woody and Monk and the one and only Satchmo. But they're all still with us, too. We see and hear them in our mind's eye all the time. We remember the ballrooms and the big bands, the clubs and small groups. Wish they were here, but they too have moved on some time ago. Loved hearing those sounds. There was an 'air' about bands. There was an excitement. Remember how it felt? I do. What was going on… The intensity building as the band set up. Forget the miles they or you drove to get there. You greet friends, small talk a little, and finally show time! NOW! The lights come down…the noise fades and BAM! The air bursts open with new sounds. Fast sound, slow sound, frantic sound, blue sound…it was fantastic!"

It's the reason Texas bandleader Alan Glasscock and others insist the big bands never left. "They didn't leave at all. Only the audience left! But that seems to be changing, thanks to the amazing generation of younger people who are becoming fans of big band music and swing dancing. The future of swing music is firmly in their hands," he told me "When I first began listening to big band music while in elementary school in the mid-70s, my peers thought the music sounded weird. The generation grew up on KISS and AC/DC and they couldn't understand my fascination with that genre. But equally important is hearing a live big band…in person! Nothing beats it. I've turned on a lot of younger people to swing music just by hearing my band in person."

In 1934 when Benny Goodman returned from a disastrous west coast trip which turned around at the Palomar Ballroom in Los Angeles, he fueled an overnight growth in the popularity of swing music when his "Let's Dance" program began. It was first broadcast on NBC as a five-hour program, that would be unheard of today, and it was sponsored by National Biscuit Company. The bands? Goodman, Kel Murray and Latin king Xavier Cugat were chosen to headline a full three hour segment which cleverly used the time zones to headline different bands. It started on Saturday, Dec. 1 at 10:30 p.m. (EST) and continued westward on the hour. In your mind you can see couples rolling up the rugs to get ready for their own dance marathon!

Goodman's segment, said music critic George Simon, was "downright thrilling."

The use of Fletcher Henderson, his black arranger and about 70 swing charts he had written, were the feature that impressed listeners. In less than a year, a labor dispute at Nabisco ended the program and it never returned. Ironically, Cugat and Murray's society orchestra were given the first two "live" hours of the broadcast and Goodman wasn't on until the last hour much later in

Benny Goodman Poster   Photo courtesy of Buckeye Lake (OH) Museum

the evening in the east. However, reviewers and listeners believed Goodman was the best part of the broadcast and the network never changed the alignment. Benny's bookings jumped as the swing fans around the country heard his music. Its beginning is still sketchy but radio remotes and experimental programming started shortly after KDKA, Pittsburgh, gave us regular broadcasting in 1920.

But getting the remote done in those days was more complicated than simply making a phone call and amplifying it.

It meant getting a telephone line installed, having a special microphone which was usually a large round head that held the mike by springs and getting the band grouped around it to ensure some kind of sound balance. It required an engineer and an announcer to get it on the air. The networks didn't "mike" sections of the band as they do today but engineers knew getting musicians close to a large stationery object in the middle created acceptable sound at the time. According to *Wikipedia*, the earliest remote was probably the Waldorf Astoria Orchestra playing at the hotel of the same name in 1923. A year later, the Oriole Orchestra of Dan Russo and Ted Fio Rito put Chicago on the map for dance band listeners in the Midwest when the group opened the ritzy Edgewater Beach Hotel to an extended radio audience.

Another first in band remotes occurred in 1925 when another jointly led band—the Carleton Coon and Joe Sanders Orchestra—played a gig relayed from the Muehbach Hotel in Kansas City to a regional audience. You had to love late hours to hear the Coon-Sanders band; its music was broadcast from midnight on. From that first broadcast, the band decided on another name: the Kansas City Night Hawks.

My first memories of great bands of the period I never saw but heard came from east coast locations that took on a life of their own to me. I can still picture the old wicker chairs as my dad and I sat in front of the Philco in the dining room of a cottage at Buckeye Lake, OH on weekends just enjoying the sounds. The Waldorf-Astoria Hotel, of course, was the sponsor of a number of big band broadcasts. Some will remember the broadcasts of Artie Shaw from the Rose Room of Boston's Ritz Carlton Hotel and CBS announcers "bringing you the music of Count Basie and his Orchestra coming from the Famous Door on 52nd Street, New York City." Probably the one I remember best is former bandleader Frank Dailey who owned the Meadowbrook "on Route 23 just off the Pompton Turnpike in Cedar Grove, New Jersey." The music magazine Downbeat would monthly tell readers where big bands were booked and the Meadowbrook was one of the most popular listings.

Another site not too far away was the Glen Island Casino. Veteran announcer Hugh James, who radio listeners heard on the program *Big Town* with Edward G. Robinson and later in the mid-1950s on a show called *Concerning Miss Marlowe* was at the Casino May 17, 1939, the night Glenn Miller's popular band finished a series of sellout performances ending with the casino. James opened the radio show telling an NBC audience "Good evening ladies and gentlemen, the spotlight is on celebrities and music at the Glen Island Casino as it opens its 1939 season…Let's listen to the music of Glenn Miller and his orchestra…"

The spring and fall of 1939 were the best times for Glenn and the revitalized Miller band. His first band had failed, Glenn later admitted, because it had no identifying or distinctive sound. Benny Goodman later in life told the story that Glenn visited him while both bands were playing Dallas and he was quite disillusioned. "He asked me what do you do? How do you make it? I told him 'I don't know, Glenn…you just stay with it."

Fortunately both did. For Miller, the Glen Island Casino gig capped a tour that included the Meadowbrook, the NY State Fair in Syracuse (where it was the largest gathering a big band ever had at the time), a sold out Hershey, PA and the band cruised into Carnegie Hall for a concert along with other mainliners like Paul Whiteman, Goodman and Fred Waring.

Days later, the band signed a contract with Chesterfield Cigarettes to broadcast from wherever it was to do a 15 minute show weekly! Don't forget this was the era before tape delays! Said saxophonist Willie Schwartz, whose clarinet created the sound Glenn had been searching for, the hectic schedule of gigs, radio shows, travel and personal appearances actually put the band in a railroad boxcar once to do a live radio broadcast! Longtime bassist Trigger Alpert probably summed it up best: "Miller had America's music pulse… He knew what would please listeners." But what probably pleased Glenn secretly was knowing that acclaimed trumpeter Louis Armstrong carried seven inch reel to reel tapes of the Miller band's 33 and 78 inch recordings when he toured. That's adolation.

It was the difference between success and starvation in a stressful American era. Pianist Jess Stacy said the Benny Goodman band would do 50 straight one nighters going from New Jersey to North Carolina and then back to Pennsylvania. Buddy Rich and Woody Herman, two seasoned veterans of the road, would continue the exhaustive grind long after Benny died.

Was there spiritual help for musicians? It came later. The Jazz Ministry of Saint Peter's Lutheran Church of New York City celebrates a ministry of love and the joy of beautiful music by holding a worship service featuring name and aspiring artists past and present. The Jazz Ministry at Saint Peter's Church was founded in 1965 by the late John Garcia Gensel who crafted the important element of this service; the Jazz Vespers.

It takes a step into a city where the crassness and gaudiness of the places where musicians worked would hardly suggest that God was or is present. Said the Rev. Dale Lind of Saint Peter's not long ago in a Jazz Appreciation Month explanation: "The Jazz Ministry has given musicians opportunities of love, understanding and acceptance. The highly personalized pastoral services provide emotional and spiritual support, through counseling musicians, their families and friends in homes, clubs, hospitals or wherever needed. Pastor Lind presides at marriages, baptisms, funerals and memorial celebrations of the lives of musicians." Swing musicians know and love Christ the Lord, too.

While swing/jazz was vogue and the beat was pulsing other leaders found popular songs could generate the same feeling thanks to a ready made beat. Artie Shaw made his first public appearance as a bandleader and clarinet in 1936 at a swing concert at Broadway's Imperial Theater. An unknown at the time, he found an enthusiastic audience and a few years later, he recorded his famous hit *Begin the Beguine*. He later joked that it was a "nice little tune from one of Cole Porter's very few flop shows." Fame came quickly. He was dubbed "King of Swing," a title both Benny and Paul Whiteman had worn for a while too.

While the struggle is to keep big band music alive, it's noticeable that seniors continue to love to hear it. Steve Cooper, a Chicago bandleader who continues to focuses on original music from the great dance bands such as Eddie Howard, Dick Jurgen's, Freddy Martin, Jan Garber, Sammy Kaye, Bob Crosby, Chuck Foster, Henry Jerome and Red Nichols and the Five Pennies, also does one man video shows for libraries and senior centers throughout the Midwest showing rare videos of the heyday of big bands. "The show is so popular I've done over 130 shows in a few years," he says. [7]

So do drummers have all the fun?

I answered that question as a 17-year-old in a pick up band playing a holiday gig in northern Ohio. We had just set up and we were having a smoke when an older friend of the leader of our group came up and began talking about how he missed the old days of playing in a house band both men belonged to in the city. A few minutes later, the leader asked me if I minded if his friend "sat in" for some numbers. But, he told me, not to worry… You can eat his dinner and sit with his wife," he smiled. An attractive woman twice my age, I not only ate his dinner, his wife and I danced a few times though we didn't have much conversation. I finished the night by playing one set and got an evening's pay!

1. www.thesession.org/discussions/display/7222comments
2. www.cledgriffin.fsnet.co.uk/dancing.html
3. Stephen Little, email, Dec. 19, 2001
4. http://musicmachinery.com
5. www.traditional-jazz.com/mainpages/krupa.htm
6. Michael Berkowitz, email, Aug. 26, 2010
7. Steve Cooper, email, Aug. 12, 2010

Theme Songs
of the Big Bands

Some bandleaders thought theme songs before they decided on the name of their orchestra. Others were so anxious to play first gigs they used any number of beginning or opening songs. But theme songs frequently marketed bands during the early years of the big band era. Without any marketing research advice or web sources to tell them, they played hunches about how they could influence a public they didn't know statistically. Themes did identify the major bands and groups. The competition for bands was keen and themes became identifying musical logos. Noticeably, in the 1920s and 30s, musical organizations were known as orchestras. It was a formal title because most musical groups were formally dressed for their gigs which weren't called "gigs" either. They were performances or engagements. By the 1940s, the term "band" became prevalent in describing groups like Benny Goodman, Fletcher Henderson, Harry James and other organizations. Informality and slang were already vogue. Several lists of themes were included in my first book, *Big Band Days: A Memoir and Source Book (2003)* and other references included Jimmie R. Gibbons' compilation in the *Browsers, December, 2004*; Leo Walker, *The Big Band Almanac (revised) 1989*; Steve Knopper, *Swing! The Essential Album Guide, 1999* and an extensive listing at Christopher Popa's *Big Band Library.com*.

Theme parties have become popular and big band opening songs have been a natural topic. Each generation can have its own party theme; for example, older generations of music lovers would probably like Depression Era band themes while baby boomers would more likely enjoy an Awesome 80s Theme Gala. You might have difficulty getting a 70 or 80 year old to understand a melody played by the Doobies like *Jesus Is Just Alright* or *Rockin' Down the*

Highway. Hosts have spent time in flea markets to find memories of the past to fit the party. Some hosts, I'm told, ask guests to bring family memories; photos, memorabilia and bits and pieces from the community or neighborhood. All that is left is to get a CD player and a batch of vintage disks that you can also find at a flea market or Walmart or even Barnes & Noble or Borders.

But you need a starting point and what better than a list of the big bands over the years and their theme songs. Here's a partial list of big band era theme songs, the bands and the year the songs were recorded.

A

And the Angels Sing, Ziggy Elman Band, late 1940s
Auld Lang Syne, Guy Lombardo Orchestra, early 1920s
Alexander's Singing, Van Alexander Orchestra, 1938
A Kiss From Me to You, Ray Pearl Orchestra, 1937
Anita, Skitch Henderson Band, 1947
Ain't Misbehavn', Fats Waller Orchestra, 1932
Angry, Tiny Hill Orchestra, 1933
Artistry in Rhythm, Stan Kenton Band, 1941
After Hours, Ted G. Buckner Band, 1946
Arsenic and Old Lace, Jerry Jerome Band, 1942
A-Tisket, A-Tasket, Ella Fitzgerald, 1938
Amazing Grace, When the Saints Come Marching In, medley, Don Cantwell, The Cliff Dwellers, 1991
Apurksody, Starburst, Gene Krupa Orchestra with Mike Berkowitz, 1930s
And Then Some, Ozzie & Harriet Nelson Orchestra, 1935
Angelina, Louie Prima Band, 1944

B

Blue Light, Bob Astor Band, 1940
Blue Flame, Woody Herman Orchestra, 1936
Blue Mood, Teddy Powell Orchestra, 1939
Busybody, Hal Pruden Band, 1946
Blue Rey, Nighty-Night, Alvino Rey Orchestra, 1939
Blue Nocturne, Dick Stabile Orchestra, 1936
Bubbles in the Wine, Lawrence Welk Orchestra, 1925
Billy, Billy Bishop Orchestra, 1931
Boston Tea Party, Mal Hallett Orchestra, 1920s
Breezing With the Breeze, Lou Breeze Orchestra, mid-1930s
Body and Soul, Coleman Hawkins Orchestra, 1938

Business on the O, Archie Bleyer Orchestra, late 1930s

Blue Sonata, Sonny Burke Orchestra, 1938

Bye Bye Blues, Bert Lown Orchestra, 1938

Blue Shadows, Dick Barne Orchestra

Blue Moon, George Ames Orchestra

Bei Mit Bist Du Schon, the Andrews Sisters

Body and Soul, Johnny Green Orchestra

Begin the Beguine, Eddy Haywood Band, 1940

Blue Rhythm Fantasy, Teddy Hill Orchestra

Beans and Cornbread, Louie Jordan and his Tympany Five, 1946

Bad Habits, Boyd Senter Orchestra, 1930s

Blossoms, Tony Pastor Orchestra

Tony Pastor
Photo courtesy of Lou DiSario

C

Cherokee, Redskin Rhumba, I Lost Another Sweetheart, Make Believe Ballroom, Skyline Charlie, Charlie Barnet Band, 1936-1947

Contrasts, Jimmy Dorsey Orchestra, 1935

Coral Reef, Neal Hefti Band, 1951

Careless, Eddie Howard Band, 1942

Ciribiribin, Harry James Orchestra, 1939

City Night, Jack Jenny Orchestra, 1939

Cocktails for Two, Spike Jones Band, early 1940s

Call of the Wild, Jerry Wald Band, 1941

Carla, Trumpeter's Lullaby, Ralph Martiere Orchestra, 1946

Christopher Columbus, Fletcher Henderson Band, 1946

Cherry Pink, Apple Blossom White, Prez Prado Band, 1948

Can't We Be Friends?, Johnny Messner Orchestra, 1930s

Chant of the Weed, Don Redman Orchestra, early 1930s

Commanderism, Irving Aaronson Orchestra, 1925

Cuban Pete, Tabu, Desi Arnez Orchestra

Carry Me Back to Old Virginny, Ace Brigode Band

California Here I Come, The Californians, Abe Lyman Orchestra

Cuddle Up a Little Closer, Henry Halstead Orchestra

Chris and His Gang, Horace Henderson Band

Churchmouse on a Spree, Milt Herth Band

Charm, Freddy Hinkel Orchestra

Cumana, Barclay Allen Orchestra

Clouds, Until the Real Thing Comes Along, Andy Kirk Orchestra

D

Dance of the Blue Devils, Leap Frog, Les Brown Orchestra, 1938

Danny Boy, Bobby Byrne Orchestra, 1939

Dipsy Doodle, My Reverie, Larry Clinton Orchestra, 1938

Desert Serenade, Jerry Gray Band, 1945

Doodletown Fifers, Sauter-Finegan Orchestra, 1952

Daydreams Come True at Night, Dick Jurgens Orchestra, 1939

Drifting and Dreaming I Love You, Orrin Tucker Orchestra, early 1930s

Does Your Heart Beat For Me?, Russ Morgan Orchestra, 1935

Deep Forest, Cavernous, Earl "Father" Hines Orchestra, 1928

Doodle-Doo-Doo, Art Kassell Orchestra, 1924

Dreams of You, Frank Bettencourt Band, 1962

Daybreak Serenade, Jess Stacy Orchestra, 1939

Dark Eyes, Bernie Cummins Orchestra

Don't Forget, Eddie Derange Orchestra

Dream Awhile, Frank DeVol Orchestra

Darling, Zinn Arthur Orchestra

E

East St. Louis Toodle-oo, Take the A Train, Duke Ellington Orchestra, 1920

Elks Parade, Bobby Sherwood Band, 1941

Eight Bars in a Search for Melody, Will Hudson Orchestra, 1938

Embraceable You, Bobby Hackett Orchestra, 1938

Edgar Steps Out, Edgar Hayes Orchestra

Easy to Love, My Blue Heaven, Red Sievers Orchestra, early 1930s

F

Flying Home, Lionel Hampton Band, 1940

Farmer in the Dell, Willie Farmer Band

Fascination, Will Bradley Orchestra, 1930s

Florida, the Moon and You, Ernie Hoist Orchestra

Forbidden Melody, Marvin Frederic Orchestra

For Dancers Only, Jimmy Lunceford Orchestra, 1930s

G

Gotta Have Your Love, Ina Ray Hutton Orchestra, 1924

Good Evening, Del Courtney Orchestra, 1933

Gonna Fly Now, Maynard Ferguson Band
Giannina Mia, Singing In The Wind, Ralph Flanagan Band, 1946
Got a Date With An Angel, Skinnay Ennis Orchestra, 1930s
Got a Date With An Angel, Hal Kemp Orchestra, 1930s

H

Hot Lips, When Day Is Done, Henry "Hot Lips" Busse Orchestra, 1931
Heart to Heart, Elliot Lawrence Band, 1944-45
Howdy Friends, Ray McKinley Band, 1948
Holiday Forever, Randy Brooks Band, 1945
Heart of My Heart, Sophisticated Swing, Les Elgart Band, 1945
How I Miss You When Summer Is Gone, Hal Kemp Orchestra, 1925
How Could You Forget?, Will Hollander Orchestra
Hooray for Hollywood, Jimmy "Scat" Davis Orchestra

I

I've Got a Right to Know, Georgie Auld Band, 1940
I Wish You Love, Jack Palmer Band, 1950s
I Can't Get Started With You, Bunny Berigan Orchestra, 1937
I'm Getting Sentimental Over You, Tommy Dorsey Orchestra, 1935
I've Got a Date With An Angel, Skinnay Ennis Orchestra, 1938
It's That Time Again, Buddy Morrow Band, 1947
It's A Lonesome Old Town, Jimmy Palmer Band, 1945
It's A Lonesome Old Town, Au Revoir, Pleasant Dreams, Ben Bernie Orchestra, 1921
I've Got a Right to Sing the Blues, Jack Teagarden Orchestra, 1938
I Want to Be Happy, Dick Wickman Band, 1941
I Love You, Oh, How I Love You, Tommy Tucker Orchestra, 1928
I Love You In My Dreams, Horace Heidt Orchestra, 1923
If Stars Could Talk, Nat Brandwynne Orchestra, mid-1930s
I'm Looking Over a Four-Leaf Clover, Art Mooney Band, 1940s
It's All Over Because We Are Through, Willie Bryant Band
I Want to Linger, Peter Daley Band
I Want to be Happy, Happy Felton Band
It Isn't Fair, Richard Himber Band
I Would Be Anything For You, Claude Hopkins Band
In A Mist, Bix Beiderbecke Orchestra, 1927
I Cried For You, Abe Lyman Orchestra, 1931
Imagination, Roger Wolfe Kahn Orchestra, 1932
I Never Know, Sam Donahue Orchestra

It Must Have Been a Dream, Les Hite Orchestra

J

Jazznocracy, Uptown Blues, Jimmy Lunceford Orchestra, 1927
Jumping with Symphony Sid, Tiny Kahn Orchestra
Jumping at the Savoy, Al Cooper Orchestra

K

Kaye's Melody, Sammy Kaye Orchestra, 1930s

L

Let's Dance, Benny Goodman Orchestra, 1934
Listen to My Music, Ted Heath Band, England, 1944
Lean Baby, Billy May Band, 1952
Love Thy Neighbor, Paul Neighbors Band, 1948
Last Night, Joe Venuti Orchestra, 1932
Love Rides On the Moon, Lou Bring Band
Love Me Tonight, Don Chiesta Band
Low Down Rhythm In A Top Hat, I Donahue Band
Laura, Errol Garner Trio
Let's Dance and Dream, Music in the Moonlight, Jimmy Grier Orchestra, 1932
Love Letters in the Sand, George Hall Band
Let's Get Together, Chick Webb Orchestra, 1930s
Little Jazz, Roy Eldridge Band
Let's Have a Jubilee, Way Down Yonder in New Orleans, Louis Prima Orchestra

M

Melancholy Mood, Teddy Phillips Band, 1944
My Sweetheart, Paul Pendarvis Orchestra, 1930s
Mr and Mrs. Swing, Red Norvo Band, 1940
My Day Begins and Ends with You, Henry King Orchestra, early 1930s
My Time Is Your Time, Rudy Vallee Orchestra, early 1930s
Moonlight on Melody Hill, Boyd Raeburn Band, 1944
Moonlight Serenade, Glenn Miller Orchestra, 1937
Moonlight Serenade, Tex Beneke Band, 1946
Memories of You, Sonny Dunham Band, 1940
Melancholy Lullaby, Malibu, Benny Carter Orchestra, 1933
Minnie the Moocher, Cab Calloway Orchestra, 1928
My Shawl, Xavier Cugat Orchestra, 1932-33

Moon Mist, Ectasy, Hal McIntyre Band, 1941

Memories of You, Memo Bernabei Band, 1958

Midnight, Joe Haymes Orchestra, 1932

My Bill, Bill Clifford Band, 1941

My Twilight Dream, Eddie Duchin Orchestra, 1932

My Twilight Dream, Eddie Duchin Orchestra, 1962

My Heart Stood Still, Tweet Hagan Band

My Promise to You, Larry Green Band

My Old Kentucky Home, Johnny Hamp Orchestra

My Dear, Jan Garber Orchestra

My Sentimental Heart, Carmen Cavallaro Orchestra, 1939

Moonlight on the Ganges, Harry Candulla Orchestra

Monmarte Rose, Keith Beecher Band

Music In My Fingers, Ray Block Orchestra

My Colleen, Bobby Byrne Orchestra

Moon River, Henry Mancini Orchestra, 1961

Music in the Moonlight, Jimmy Grier Orchestra, 1932

Moon Over Miami, Dean Hudson Orchestra

My Isle of Golden Dreams, Phil Spitalny and his All-Girl Orchestra,

My Buddy, Buddy Rogers Orchestra

N

No Foolin', Lennie Herman Band, early 1950s

Nightmare, Artie Shaw Orchestra, 1936-37

Nola, Vincent Lopez Orchestra, 1917

Night Must Fall, Dick Trimble Orchestra, Lancaster, OH early 1930s

Night Is Gone, Nice People, Henry Jerome Orchestra, early 1930s

Nighthawk Blues, Coon-Sanders Orchestra

Night Of Love, Emil Flindt Orchestra

Night Train, Buddy Morrow Band, 1950

O

On The Track, Ferde Grofe Orchestra

One Minute to One, Gray Gordon Orchestra

Oh You Beautiful Doll, Chuck Foster Band, 1940

One O'Clock Jump, Count Basie Orchestra, 1935

Oh Look At Me Now, Joe Bushkin Band, 1951

Out of the Night, Ted Weems Orchestra, 1923

On the Sunny Side of the Street, When It's Sleepy Time Down South,

Louie Armstrong Orchestra, 1930s

P

Piano Portrait, Jack Fina Band, 1946

Pastoral Blossoms, Tony Pastor Orchestra, early 1930s

Pipe Dreams, Tommy Reynolds Orchestra, 1939

Pipe Dreams, Dick Fidler Band, 1952

Pagan Moon, Ted Black Orchestra, 1929

Pretty Little Petticoat, Raymond Scott Orchestra, 1939

Prisoner of Love, Russ Columbo Orchestra, 1931

Tommy Reynolds
Photo courtesy of Lou DiSario

Q

Quaker City Jazz, Jan Savitt Orchestra, 1935

R

Rippling Rhythm, Shep Fields Orchestra, 1929

Racing with the Moon, Vaughn Monroe Band, 1940

Relaxing at the Touro, Mugsy Spanier Band, 1941

Romance, Ray Herbeck Orchestra, 1935

Rose Room, That's What I Like About the South, Phil Harris Orchestra, 1930s

Red Rose, Francis Craig Orchestra

Rio Rita, Ted Fio Rito Orchestra

Rose Room, Art Hickman Orchestra, 1920s

Rhapsody in Blue, Paul Whiteman Orchestra, 1930s

S

Sleepy Alto, Johnny Bothwell Band, 1946

Slow But Sure, Charley Agnew Orchestra, 1934

Sunrise Serenade, Frankie Carle Band, 1944

Sometimes I'm Happy, Blue Barron Orchestra, 1936

Sing, Sing, Sing, Way Down Yonder in New Orleans, Louie Prima Orchestra, early 1930s

Sunset Serenade, Art Mooney Orchestra, late 1930s

Swing Out, Tuxedo Junction, Erskine Hawkins Orchestra, 1939

Summertime, Big Crosby, 1938

Slumber, Sun Burst, Bob Chester Band, 1942

Say it With Music, Sweet and Lovely, Gus Arnheim Orchestra

Strange Cargo, Freddie Slack Band, 1942

Star Dreams, Charley Spivak Band, 1940

Snowfall, Claude Thornhill Band, 1940

Summertime, Bob Crosby Band, 1942

Song Of the Islands, Ben Pollack Orchestra 1925

Sugar Blues, Clyde McCoy Orchestra, 1920

Skater's Waltz, Barney Rapp Orchestra, early 1920s

Soft, Gravy Train, Tiny Bradshaw Orchestra, 1933

Smoke Rings, Glen Gray Orchestra, 1930s

Seems Like Old Times, Arthur Godfrey, Archie Bleyer Orchestra, 1945

Shine On Harvest Moon, Jimmy Joy Orchestra

Scatterbrain, Frankie Masters Orchestra

Sleep, Fred Waring Orchestra

T

Think of Me, Will Bradley Band, 1941

Things Aren't What They Used to Be, Monk Rowe Band, 1990s

The Chapel in the Moonlight, You Can Call It Madness, If I Ever Love Again,
    Russ Carlyle Band, 1940

Times Square Scuttle, Lenny Hayton Orchestra, 1937

Thankful, Teddy Phillips Band, 1946

Two Clouds in the Sky, Tommy Reed Band, 1946

Thinking of You, Kay Kyser Orchestra, 1930s

The Very Thought of You, Ray Noble Orchestra, 1927

The Waltz You Saved For Me, Wayne King Orchestra, 1927

Tonight We Love, Freddie Martin Orchestra 1934

Tonal Color Serenade, Bob Strong Band, 1943

Teach Me To Smile, I'm Not Forgetting, Don Bestor Orchestra, 1921

Tarantula, Ambrose and his Orchestra

The Moon Is Low, Dale Brodie Band

Tonight There Is Music, Smith Ballew Orchestra

Three Shades of Blue, Del Courtney Orchestra

The Sandman, The Dorsey Brothers Band

The White Star of Sigma Nu, Johnny Long Orchestra, 1930s

The Gentleman Waits, Will Osborne Orchestra

U

Up A Lazy River, Si Zentner Band, 1957

Until the Best Thing Comes Along, Andy Kirk Orchestra, 1929

Under the Stars, Jack Denny Orchestra

V

Vieni Su, Carl Ravazza Band, 1940

W

What's New? Moonlight in Vermont, Billy Butterfield Band, 1945
Was I to Blame for Falling in Love With You? Smoke Rings, Glen Gray Orchestra, 1930s
Wailing to the Four Winds, Red Nichols Orchestra 1923
When the Lights Go On Again, Lucky Millender Band, 1940
When Romance Calls, Leon Belasco Orchestra, 1936
When My Baby Smiles at Me, Ted Lewis Orchestra, 1916
Weary, Gill Emerson Orchestra
We'll Recapture the Moment, Dick Gasparre Orchestra

Y

Young Man With a Horn, Ray Anthony Band, 1946
You Call It Madness I Call It Love, Don Glasser Orchestra, 1938
You Are My Lucky Star, Enoch Light Orchestra, 1929
You Go to My Head, Mitchell Ayers Orchestra, 1935
You're Just a Dream From True, Isham Jones Orchestra, 1919

Reminisces

of the Big Band Days

Big band days were around for such a short time yet the memories of those who danced to them, played in the bands or just enjoyed the sounds live on.

Later generations are sometimes puzzled by the value and intimacy of such a brief period of history forgetting that war and the threat of war enveloped the big band era from start to finish.

Go to a nursing home near you and talk to any resident 65 and over and I think you'll get a story or two about personal experiences that came from the period and the music. I continue to do that and I enjoy the nuances of those who witnessed the pain and passion and the interludes of wonderful music. It's truly an education.

Listen to John Ghrist of WDCB, Chicago who says "I am too young (61) to remember the heyday of the big bands but grew up listening to my folk's 78 RPM records. My parents went dancing to places like Madura's Danceland in Hammond, IN. In the 1970s and early '80s there were still big band tunes on the Top 40. I was working at several easy listening stations and I never realized that someday I would be the only big band DJ left in Chicago. But I'm doing my best to keep the big bands on the air."

The younger you are the more the stories of those who lived in the 40s, 50s and even 60s can be captivating. The sacrifices of the Greatest Generation, the emotional love stories, the desire to get past where they were, the fear of the future they faced but how the music (big band) soothed them. A great number of novels came from such plots and without a doubt, a large vault of film based upon the 1940s and 50s offered Ted Turner's enterprise years of movie titles.

The late Dave Garroway, a radio and TV host and onetime disc jockey. explained how the 1940s affected him. "When I came back from the war the band that played the blues was a band that could now blow you away literally and physically. Woody Herman's first Herd had more power than I ever heard before. It was a band that could be heard and seen live… radio didn't do it justice I thought. I was working a station and when Woody came on I had to turn the gain down cause it would drive those in the front row out of their seats." It was 1946, the year Woody made his first million payroll.[1]

And a later day bandleader, Alan Glasscock of Texas, identifies with those images and sounds of the past. "My musicians are somewhat amazed at how technically demanding playing the old big band charts can be, especially when they heretofore mocked the Glenn Miller style, thinking it was very vanilla and boring. That is until they played the original charts!" Alan said. "They have a new found respect for this antique music and they know they have to be on their toes when reading down some of these charts especially when I call up Miller's *Anvil Chorus* or Goodman's *Mission to Moscow* on a gig!"

Attitude as in any creative enterprise makes the difference. Says Alan: "I believe that leading a band was what I was put on this earth to do. No question about it. I do sometimes worry that at some point our audience will literally die off and then no one will want to hear this great style of music anymore. But then when we play our annual 'hangar dance fundraiser for a local aviation museum in which we draw 800 to 1200 people every year — and about one third of them are under age 39 — I get rejuvenated and we keep on swingin'!"

Yet, he also remembers his peers as he grew up and began identifying with music they thought quaint. "My peers thought the music (big band) sounded weird (an ironic comment from the generation that grew up on KISS and AC/DC) and they couldn't understand my fascination with that genre. I found over the years that the primal recording methods available during the big band era had a lot to do with recent generations appreciating this style. I've had many people tell me that hearing a live band in person makes all the difference and I agree! Nothing beats standing in front of a band of 17 musicians and hearing all those great sounds come alive again! I've turned on a lot of younger people to swing music just by hearing my band in person." [2]

Again, John offers a perspective from his work at WDCB which broadcasts from the College of DuPage in Glen Ellyn near Chicago: "Midwest Ballroom (his program) was created to get the big bands back on the radio.

These are the fine local and territory orchestras that my listeners can go and see and dance to. I have taken on this volunteer show to actively promote them and even emcee their summer park concerts. Years ago, there used to be lots of live remotes on Chicago radio. The old bands are nice, but they are gone now. We need to promote the big bands that are still performing and keeping this great music available to the public and new generations of listeners. It seems that the only place to hear the really good orchestras is on public radio."

Like others, especially those who are older, it's a mystery why big bands have been ignored by many AM and even niche FM stations. "I just don't get it. We can pull in over 2,000 people to a free park concert without any problems with a good sounding big band. The young people who run these events will turn around and still hire rock bands and CD spinners who attract much smaller audiences and create trouble in the parks. It does not make any sense," John says.

The music and musicians were the attraction but it was the ballrooms that brought people together. "Ballrooms have an ambiance that other contemporary structures fail to achieve. A ballroom was designed to hold large crowds. There is just something about a large crowd sharing an exciting experience. As a ballroom operator these magical moments can give you a chill. It's not the same as a concert or some other experiences. In the ballroom, you are a participant not a spectator, " said John Matter, a longtime Iowa ballroom owner and president

Matter's Ballroom Photo courtesy of John Matter (NBEA)

of the National Ballroom & Entertainment Assn (NBEA). Ballrooms offered the space for dancing that listeners craved and it elicited the response from audiences that promoters and owners loved to see and hear.

They also created the need for their own code of informal conduct, too. A Web site called *The Satin Ballroom: Swing Etiquette*, provided some details on how dancers should behave.

The necessity, said the web site, comes from dealing with inconsiderate people. "We are not quite as stuffy, but our dance floor is usually packed exactly like ballrooms in the old days. No wonder they invented the Balboa here in California. What was different back then was that people respected each other and each other's space more."

A major complaint? People standing around on the ballroom floor, talking or sipping their drinks. They can crowd an already crowded floor and disrupt dancing.

Another constant complaint is inconsiderate people who show little regard for people around them when kicking and stepping out. You need to keep to the basics and remain in your own space…the Charleston kick can be a shin bruise or worse if you're not careful of who is close by. Nothing worse than a couple doing the Charleston, another doing the Foxtrot and a third couple doing the jitterbug in close quarters. And beginners need to re-member that *Cat's Corner* is a place reserved for the best dancers to hang out. "Beginners and intermediates should not dance there!"

What about those dancers who liked to go airborne during fast dances?

Many clubs forbade the so-called "air steps" for security reasons as well as safety. Satin Ballroom said it asked patrons to be responsible and use good judgment. It also asked that partners should make sure that both have done aerial routines before they come to the ballroom…and be absolutely sure of their moves.

Equally important, ballroom management added, is to let the band know your approval with applause. Said the ballroom: "They are not just playing for money! Particularly at the Satin Ballroom. Each of them gives the very best. Please show respect and appreciation and cheer the band on! The more you applaud, the better they will feel and play!" As a former player I applaud the reminder.

To ensure that etiquette was observed, the Satin Ballroom told dancers and patrons to use the following courtesy: When the male partner asked a girl to dance, it was expected that he would take responsibility for her safety and enjoyment during the dance. When she accepts your offer to dance with her, she expects you to be in charge. That includes escorting her back to her table, too.

During the dance, said the Satin Ballroom management "Don't pull her arm out and don't destroy her hairdo and makeup! Don't dip if you don't know the girl well because many women feel uncomfortable with that! Others suggest that being dipped to our right because it throws them off balance and is unnatural."

Satin Ballroom has attempted to revive the elegance and flair of the big dances of the 1930s and '40s. They ask their patrons to dress up and make such occasions special. I wish I lived near Satin Ballroom… we need such a return to the 'good ol' days of civility, fun, good music and dancing. [3]

Some years earlier, Cleveland, OH city council made sure that dancers knew that dancing too close would not be tolerated. Said Section 8 of the Cleveland ordinance: "Partners are not permitted to dance with cheeks close or touching. When dancers put their cheeks together it is simply a case of public love-making." Imagine enforcing that rule today!

Yet, the music was always the underlining theme.

Thirty-two-year-old Joe Enroughty is too young to remember the era but he's made his purpose in life to recreate what he knows of it for audiences wherever he and his band play. "I don't think the Big Band Era will ever come back like it was in it's hey day. But I think the sound of a big band will always be popular and I think there will always be a market for it. You don't know how many times I've had people come up to me and say 'Where has all this music gone? Why doesn't anyone play it anymore?' And my response is generally 'Just listen. We are playing it. And we're playing it just for you.'"

Joe learned from his mentor, Guy Lombardo, what keeps a band popular.

Guy told Christopher Popa of Big Band Library "As soon as I see that no one is getting up to dance or that there is a buzz of conversation around the room, I know they aren't listening and aren't even interested in what's being played. This, of course, is my cue to take the song out of my books."

Musicians like Chuz Alfred of Columbus, a bandleader and once a member of the Ralph Martiere Orchestra, has more personal recollections about the era.

It was a frenetic time of impulsive decisions; some good…some not so good.

"I left OSU during my senior year in 1954, grabbed Chuck Lee, the piano player, and split for Florida to put together a group. While there we met Cannonball Adderly and Nat, who were steamin' as a sextet at Porky's in Fort Lauderdale. One night they were hung for a pianist and Cannonball called me to see if Chuck could do the gig. He told me to drag my axe along and sit in. I was blowin' a King Super 20 tenor at the time and as the night went on Cannonball said he dug my sound and wanted to switch horns. So we switched and I played his Selmer for the rest of the night. He and Nat went to NYC so he could work on his master's at New York University and on their first night in town, he wound up sittin' in at the Café Bohemia on June 19, 1995, and was hired to start working at the club two days later. In 1958, I ran into Cannonball in Washington, DC when he and Coltrane, Red Garland, Philly Joe and Paul Chambers were all with Miles. On the break, Cannonball asked me if I still had that King Super 20. I said 'No, I traded it off on a Selmer Mark IV! 'Cannonball laughed and yelled 'Hey man, you really screwed me up! I'm blowin' a King now.'" [4]

Alfred returned to his hometown in Lancaster, OH in 2008 to play a nostalgic gig at a place much apart of his past; Weldon's Sip'N'Dip Dance Party. Said a party goer that July evening: "Who would have thought we'd be dancing and eating ice cream. We used to have beers between dances."

Many older Americans are upset at media for ignoring "their" music. This is where the generational struggle is most evident. Seniors want to believe such precious moments should be heard and radio stations that they rise to in the morning and go to bed with at night should respond. Of course, there are stations, both AM and FM, that capture particular big band jazz audiences in certain localities. Strangely, I find what the stations — normally PBS outlets — play isn't what mainstream seniors are necessarily interested in. Few, if any, stations play Rudy Vallee, Ted Weems, Ted Lewis, Dick Jurgens, Dick Stabile and the legions of sweet bands that dominated the 1930s, 40s and 50s. They don't even play Glenn Miller these days! Ask a disk jockey today and you'd probably get a blank stare about sweet bands. Stations subscribe to services that basically provide jazz because they can 1. find such artists and CDs still being sold at Barnes & Noble, Borders and elsewhere, 2. announcers are familiar with Charley Parker, Dizzy Gillespie and other legendary names and play and replay their sides and 3. say broadcast people I talked to, no one at most stations hear or see demand for such music. Furthermore, few station deejays grew up with such music!

For 10 years I hosted a radio roundtable half hour on an all news station that shuffled me to different times of the weekend. We were at the whim of program directors who came and went. I had to selectively incorporate big band as a feature but run talk interviews. My engineer and I felt we had a growing audience (mostly elders) but the station wasn't interested.

Gordon Goodwin and the Big Phat Band   Photo by Glen LaFerman

While World War II, Korea and Vietnam continue to be revisited, only public broadcasting has seen fit to air much of Ken Burns' specials on the music of the period. Burns, of course, calls his programs "jazz," again missing the mark with people who vividly remember the dance music of their era. Consequently, such music simply is lost. The attitude is unless it's Glenn Miller, it doesn't exist.

An older friend, Alex Hart, formerly of Lancaster, OH, emailed me a few years ago after my *Big Bands & Great Ballrooms: America Is dancing… Again* book was published to say how much he enjoyed Kay Kyser, Ginny Sims and Harry Babbit. He told a nostalgic story about his music past. "In 1940 Rosemary (his late wife) and I had little money but we made a furniture purchase at Sears in the Pittsburgh area and one of our items was a radio that played AM and FM and recordings. It made the difference! We listened to that great music all the time. I am still listening today. We have a wonderful FM station in the Naples, (FL) area that plays 'oldies' 24 hours a day. They offer three straight hours of jazz on Sunday mornings from 9 to noon. I have to miss most of that because of church but I can usually catch the last half hour and soak up the wonderful music they play."

Alex's memories of Kay Kyser brought back thoughts about a trumpet player who became a vocalist thanks to Kay. Jimmy Palmer, said Steve Cooper, who likes to say that he has one of the most popular ballroom bands in the country, sent me a nostalgic email about Jimmy's life in the "business."

"He started his 1st band of note around the middle 1940s. Around 1950 he started playing in the style of Kay Kyser," Steve said. "He always had two (later three) trumpets, two trombones, and four saxes plus rhythm. The saxes were voiced to often sound like five saxes. His theme was *It's A Lonesome Old Town* which was Ben Bernie's theme. His gimmick was *Put on Your Dancin' Shoes* and there were sound effects like feet dancing. He had the singing song titles like Sammy Kaye and his arrangers for all those Kyser type tunes was Clark Smith, a first class arranger."

What people liked about Jimmy was his repertoire. "They did those old 1920s tunes but also did current titles of the day like *Unchained Melody, Oh My Papa* and other 50s hits. Jimmy kept everything bouncy sounding. He recorded a lot of 78s on the Mercury label and then did 45s and LPs. He played all the top ballrooms around the top hotels and, of course, he did all kinds of big band remotes. I heard the Palmer band while I was playing a one nighter in between Palmer and Charley Spivak. The crowd was good both nights. The crowd for us was about half of the crowds for the 'name' groups but then we were the last band of the weekend on a Sunday night. Nothing worse then playing the last night when the popular bands go first, our leader said. We did get paid."

Larry Faith's band was the favorite of the owners of the Melody Mill Ballroom in Chicago. In my opinion, he was the top ballroom band along with Lawrence Welk, Dick Jurgens, Eddie Howard, Jan Garber and others who were fantastic sweet bands," Steve told me.

In 1962, Jimmy Palmer returned to Chicago and became the house band at the Conrad Hilton. But it wasn't the same, Steve said. "He played for the ice show and dancing. However, he didn't have the great ballroom guys he had in New York and in his travels around the country. The band had a lot of great Chicago studio and jazz players but it didn't have the ballroom 'lilt' of the earlier bands. I bought his library in 1976. He hadn't played it for many years. He had all his LP albums on the wall. Said Jimmy: 'Elvis killed it for all the bands!'"[5]

And credit the stalwart survivors who endured generations of different kinds of music from rock'n'roll to hip hop and continued to play their music — swing and sweet ballads — wherever they could find audiences. One was a 96-year-old orchestra leader in Bronxville, NY. Ben Cutler, who died in 2001. He could accommodate any type of music and blend it to his orchestra and his crowds. Said the The New York Times upon his death, Ben "working in all the right places, from the Persian Room at the Plaza to the roof of the Astor Hotel… was one of New York's top four society orchestra leaders along with Lester Lanin, Meyer Davis and Bill Harrington."

The band business, without a doubt, was unlike any other that brought people together to work. The public saw glitzy ads, signs about one night appearances but unless they devoured the trade magazines they knew little if anything about the life of those who made music. While most have fond memories of dancing in a lakeside ballroom during summer months, few gave a thought to how musicians traveled 12 months a year earning a living. Weather in the northeast could disrupt or cancel events which meant money lost for all concerned. During the late 1930s, for example, Glenn Miller was having enough trouble finding the distinctive sound for his band, searching for talent and trying to pay competitive salaries when a treacherous winter storm came barreling through the northeast while the Miller group was doing one nighters from Pennsylvania to New England. On snow covered roads an accident caused a member of the band to total Glenn's car. Then two trumpet players went on a drinking binge and, meanwhile, the remaining two cars broke down stranding half of the rhythm and sax sections. The band was scheduled to play a 7 hour New Year's Eve gig and Glenn had less than half of his group assembled when he gave the downbeat. The Miller band made $200 that evening and Glenn paid off the players and folded the same night. Happy New Year!

Imagine having to be some place distant virtually every night. That's the way touring big bands met the needs of payroll and crowds of loyal fans. A popular band for dancing that incorporated novelty with its routine was Les Brown and his Band of Renown. The band stayed intact by playing grueling one nighters on the west coast and doing air checks two months out of the year while remaining based in Los Angeles at the Casino Gardens. The band played the Palladium in LA but also did trips to the Midwest to perform at the popular Aragon Ballroom in Chicago. Most of its work was private parties, prom dates, radio shows and recordings. In 1949, the band was chosen to do the sound track for the film *Young Man With A Horn*. A year later, the entire band appeared in the movie *I'll Get By*. At the same time, Les had struck up a relationship with Bob Hope and had replaced the Kenton band on the Hope radio show. When Hope went to network TV, the Les Brown band went with him. It traveled farther than it ever dreamed when it began working with Hope on his USO tours around the globe. I traveled with the entourage from Japan to South Korea during the 1950s and I have great memories of the small talk that had to be loud on a noisy C-124 aircraft.

Dick Stabile came back from the war and resumed leadership of his band thanks to his wife Grace Berrie who sang and managed the band while he was gone. He, like Artie Shaw and a number of other bandleaders, continued to lead bands in the service. He settled in Los Angeles and found work on the famous Wilshire Boulevard at Slapsie Maxie's nightclub, owned by a famous boxer. A few years later, Dick landed a gig with a then unknown comedy team that lasted 31 years…a long time in any business. The team? Jerry Lewis and Dean Martin. They performed at another Hollywood landmark, Ciro's. A smooth band which fit with entertainers or playing dance numbers, the Stabile Orchestra continued over the years by moving to New Orleans where it played the Roosevelt. After recovering from a stroke, Dick took the band to the Ambassador and the Glendora Ballrooms where he played until he died of a coronary arrest.

Of course, like so many professions, musicians came in all sorts of personalities. Mary Louise DeMott did an interesting article about a musician named Boyd Senter called "Jazzologist Supreme!" A Nebraskan, Boyd's claim to fame was giving Glenn Miller his first job in 1921. But his life in the music business was extraordinary. At 13, Boyd was considered a prodigy and the only juvenile in the country to have launched a band. He found Glenn working as a "soda jerk" in Boulder, CO and gave him a seat in the trombone section of his newly formed band although he had his doubts. "He only had two white shirts to his name and he couldn't read a note of music. But I hired him… anyway." The music business and dancers are indebted to Boyd for discovering the world's greatest bandleader.

On his way his way west, Boyd met a musical instrument manufacturer and persuaded him to give his band some instruments. A trombone was among those given and since Glenn needed an instrument, it became Glenn's. Legend has it that Glenn used that trombone until his death.

Meanwhile, Boyd continued to promote himself and his bands. By his late teens, Senter had organized and ended six different bands. He knew how to survive in the Depression. As a single or with his group, he appeared on stage and could play 33 instruments! He was paid $50 as a single for each number he played but the best days were during the 1920s when he took home $1,500 a week! He attracted all kinds of admirers. Gangster Bugs Moran liked his music and invited him to a weekend at one of his secluded mansions. He dispatched his bulletproof limo to transport Senter. According to the bandleader, mobsters liked show people. "We were in no danger. They kept us out of their business," he told DeMott. [6]

But the public could be fickle and audiences could disappear as easily as they appeared. Paul Whiteman, considered the "king of jazz," rose to the top and tried desperately to stay but failed. Most believe his title really belonged to Benny Goodman who became a phenomenon in 1935 after he and his band had appeared at the Palomar Ballroom outside of Los Angeles and drew crowds of teenagers and young adults by playing arrangements by black arranger and former bandleader Fletcher Henderson. Whiteman tried to counter Benny's "modern sounds." He revamped his style, hired new arrangers and even brought in the popular Miller group, the Modernaires, to sing with his orchestra. He disbanded once and started again only to repeat the process after he had appeared in the movie *Strike Up the Band*. After the war, he joined ABC where he conducted studio orchestras on radio and television and hosted his own program in the 1950s.

Drew Savage in a web site about *whateverhappenedtoyouknowwho* offered the best solution to those who enjoy the music of an earlier day. "For about twenty years or so, from the late nineteen fifties through the nineteen seventies, just about the only way to form an appreciation of what the big bands and dance bands of their day sounded like, was to seek their old recordings. Or, if you were really lucky, a then current version of one of the last remaining "ghost" bands might pay a visit to your town. Jimmy Dorsey, perhaps, or Harry James or Tex Beneke maybe Count Basie." That remains true today and makes flea markets more popular for those who enjoy the vintage sounds of the 30s, 40s and 50s.

To help you, here are groups that have reappeared as touring "ghost" dance bands from the 1930s, 40s and 50s that I found. There may be others but these bands have web sites:

Harry James Orchestra, www.harryjames.com; **Les Elgart Orchestra**, www.leselgart.com; **Hal McIntyre Orchestra**, www.halmcintyre.com; **Nelson Riddle Orchestra**, www.nelsonriddle.com; **Cab Calloway Orchestra**, www.cabcalloway.com; **Tommy Dorsey Orchestra**, www.tommydorsey.com; **Les Brown's Band of Renown**, www.bandofrenown.com; **Russ Morgan Orchestra**, www.russmorganorchestra.com; **Sammy Kaye Orchestra**, www.sammykayeorchestra.com; **Jimmy Dorsey Orchestra**, jimmydorseyorchestra.com; **Jan Garber Orchestra**, www.jangarber.com; **Dick Jurgens Orchestra**, www.dickjurgens.com; **Gene Krupa Orchestra**, www.berkmusic.com; **Count Basie Orchestra**, www.countbasieorchestra.com; **Duke Ellington Orchestra**, www.dukeellingtonorchestra.com; **Guy Lombardo Orchestra**, www.guylombardoorchestra.com; **Xavier Cugat Orchestra**, www.xaviercugatorchestra.com; **Glenn Miller Orchestra**, www.glennmillerorchestra.com; **Artie Shaw Orchestra**, www.artieshaworchestra.com; **Lester Lanin Orchestra**, www.lesterlaninorchestra.com; **Woody Herman Orchestra**, www.woodyherman.com

Ballroom owners had their own doubts about the big band era and their investment. An elegant nationally recognized dance hall in the west, the Crystal Ballroom in Portland, OR, was a regular on the big band trail during the 1920s, 30s, 40s and 50s and its history tells of its successes and struggles over 90 years. Said its web site: "The hall has seen countless first loves unfold, police raids, visits by silent screen idols and beat poets, psychedelic light shows, narrow escapes from fire, demolition and neglect, and a listing in the National Register of Historic Places. Today, it is a vital, thriving McMenamins which owns and operates a live music palace that hosts everything from rock'n'roll and country to hip-hop and big band swing."

Ballrooms of the early big band era were family businesses, James Ronan of Iowa Rock and Roll Music Association told me in a letter. "I missed the real big band time because I was born 1950. I saw rock, soul and

> *The hall has seen countless first loves unfold, police raids, visits by silent screen idols and beat poets, psychedelic light shows, narrow escapes from fire, demolition & neglect, and a listing in the National Register of Historic Places.*

blue bands touring in the 1960s and '70s but I remember my first ballroom concert was at Spillville, IA at the Inwood Pavilion. I was hooked on the music and the ballrooms but by 1970s, dancing fell on hard times. Concerts were in rather than dancing. These shows were in large cities and usually booked arenas not ballrooms. I have fond memories of big band and rock and roll in ballrooms though. Ballrooms, to me, were great places for families to gather and enjoy the live music in the pre-rock and roll days. The Iowa Rock and Roll Music Association has always had a goal of trying to preserve as much music from the ballrooms as possible. Both are important."

So what makes it worthwhile to the thousands of musicians, leaders and others to continue in such a risky enterprise?

Ron Smolen, a Chicago area bandleader who has been at this fun experience for years and uses the theme "Every Night Is New Year's Eve" in describing what his band can do for a party, a wedding or an event, offers this insightful assessment:

"We're standing next to the stage at a church dance on break. This lady comes over in tears looking totally anguished and asked to speak to me. Wondering if I had done something to offend this lady, several of my musicians came to back me and see what was wrong. But instead of getting yelled at, she said: 'THANK YOU! Thank you... for the wonderful music and the gift you gave me tonight.' She pointed out a young man and said he's my son. He obviously was afflicted with Downs Syndrome. 'He never dances, he never responds. He just sits there. But tonight, your music triggered something! He's dancing with me and with anyone and everyone... even strangers. Thank you! Thank you!' The feeling of satisfaction is immense!"

Ron's view has changed over the years because of the changing composition of the audiences. "It's no longer about just playing music. People look to be entertained. Thus, I attempt to create a party atmosphere at every performance. My mio is that I want everyone to feel as though they have just attended a big family wedding. At the end of the performance, during the playing of our theme song, I introduce the members of the orchestra, say goodnight to the crowd, tell all to drive home safely and I also add the following comment: 'I hope we rekindled some old memories of days gone by, and gave you some new memories to take home with you.'"

He calls his group a "variety band, a crossover band." His 10 piece orchestra performs standards, pop tunes, big band, swing, jazz and sweet numbers and it can fit into a space against the wall 12 X 16! Ron says the changing scene creates debate and criticism among musicians who are wrestling with similar issues and approach it differently.

"I have been cursed by some who feel I discredit the business one way or another by not choosing a singular direction. Although we have played hundreds of dances, I have one major dance club that will not hire us because we play a variety of styles and not just sweet or swing," he wrote me.

He insists that there is work out there if you do stay versatile and open minded and NOT choose to play only one type of music. He explains: "We've performed everything from baptisms to weddings and even divorce parties. We have also performed just about everywhere including porches, loading docks, theater stage shows, big band weekends, parade floats, summer concerts, grand openings and any event and location imaginable. We even performed Polish waltzes and Polkas inside a funeral parlor during a wake and at a grave site as the casket was lowered." [7]

Les Brown drummer Jack Sperling told me that you had to have a strong commitment to the work and the music and the staying power to endure the odd hours. "Most leaders were happy to have gigs and during lean times you appreciated the fact that you were working period. I was fortunate to be with good bands over the years and rarely had a down time," he said.

One of the most powerful stories of a handicapped musician who continued to play and travel while battling congenital tuberculosis of the spine was William Henry "Chick" Webb's 30 year struggle. He became one of New York City's most competitive drummers from a base at the Cotton Club where his band won a number of "battle of the bands" contests at Harlem's Savoy Ballroom. His style attracted the best drummers in the business, Buddy Rich and Louie Bellson and others. Because of his deformed spine, he was perched on a raised platform and used custom-made pedals and goose-neck cymbal holders and a 28-inch bass drum and a number of other percussion devices to create thundering sound. In the 1930s, he was an inspiration to other handicapped players who desperately needed a role model to lead the way.

Most current bandleaders learned by apprenticeship from past musical icons. They studied the style and music of those who toured. Leader of the well-known west coast aggregation, the Big Phat Band from Los Angeles, Gordon Goodwin, still recalls what Stan Kenton meant to him. "One of the best learning experiences of my life was attending the Stan Kenton Clinic at Redlands University when I was a kid. It did much to form my musical asthetic," he told me. If you pick up a CD called *act your age*, (Gordon Goodwin Big Phat Band, 2008) you are treated to the variety of styles and shapes of Gordon's music today.

Musicians always have fond memories of great events in which they participated. Chuz Alfred remembers playing with Ralph Martiere at a debutante ball in Houston in 1959 where he ended up jamming until dawn at the musicians' union hall. Next stop was Dallas. "We were at the Statler-Hilton I think doing the Petroleum Club party with a revolving bandstand at one end and stationery risers at the other. We alternated sets on the revolving stand with Shep Fields and the hall was so big that we could barely hear Leon Merion's Big Band at the other end featuring Charley Shavers. Believe me, there was a whole lotta of trumpetin' going on that night when Ralph, Leon and Charlie got together. But the real stars of the night were the guests themselves… the men in the latest black formal attire and their significant others all decked out in a theme of color… fusia, yellow, blue, green, orange – you name it – and it was the way… hair, hose, dress, shoes, eyeshadow to lipstick. A sparkling shower la femme with a jolt when someone grabbed you on a break and whisked you away to a hospitality room where the revelers were re-charging their batteries from the frantic energy draining goings-on in the ballroom of the battling bands!"

Sometimes, Chuz remembered, good things happened because of a chance telephone call.

Listen to Chuz relate another memorable date that occurred because he was at the right place and right time. "In June, 1986, I had been off the road since the summer of '59, finished school, married, became a daddy five times and fashioned my career in real estate. I got a call at my office from a great trumpet player from Chicago named Tommy Saunders. Tommy, in addition to his ongoing association with Wild Bill Davidson was coming to Columbus with the New McKinney's Cotton Pickers for the band's first appearance at Valley Dale Ballroom since 1934 (my mother said that she and my dad were there in 1934!) Tommy said their jazz tenor man was sick and couldn't make it from Detroit.

Chuz Alfred Promotional Poster   Photo courtesy of Chuz Alfred

Would I do the gig? I knew it would be a heavy read which I hadn't done in 25 years. I told him I'd think about it. No sooner had I finished the call with Tommy than Chuck Robinette, piano player with the Martiere band called and told me 'no buts about it… you're gonna do the gig!' Well, we did. A total blast…tough charts but a lot of solo work. And a steamboat load of licks and kicks. In the band room after the gig Chuck opened his bulging briefcase with contracts, cash and a loaded 45. We just sat there grinning at each other.

"Where had the time gone?" I asked. 'Nowhere, everywhere,' he said and he chumped down on his cigar and I lit a Marlboro. As he began counting some money, he tweaked his mustache and said: 'Yeah, man… what a gas! Come on back to Chicago with us!" I was sippin bourbon and water and stuck in a time warp. I felt like I had been there and done that in '34 when mom and dad were trippin' the light fantastic. Maybe it was the heat and humidity or that smokey little stage room or the Ol' Grandad or playing with Robinette again but I think surrealism 'sat in' during the break when I was rappin.' It was a night I never forgot."

Some hundreds of miles north of Lancaster, OH and Chuz there was a ballroom that etched a flamboyant name for itself and Michigan. It was called the *Graceland Ballroom*, and it certainly had it's own grace. It's history was another matter. Giant pine logs were used to build it in northern Ogemaw County. The lumber was cut in the area and when finished it was a 95 X 120 building with a 2,400 foot dance floor and a seating capacity of about 600. The ballroom had had plenty of features to keep the "gangsta" image alive. Mannequins were used to depict the 1920s and the people who created Chicago and Detroit.

One mannequin in 1930s' clothes looked down the ballroom carrying a Thompson machine gun to get you in the mood… if you weren't. Another display was a "concrete overcoat" which explained how bodies were boxed, weighted with cement and dumped in the Detroit River. It was place for the Purple Gang to hang out with friends. The place was actually purchased as a safe house for gang members in the 1920s. You could find Al Capone there occasionally and there was plenty of "liquid gold" to fortify everybody. And the stories about the gang's influence were everywhere. It was thought that the lumber bought for the building this 3,000 foot log palace was never paid for. We do know that gangsters loved their jazz and swing music so big bands played Graceland Ballroom and my guess was they were paid handsomely unless the owners didn't like their music! As the 30s became the 1940s, the ballroom thrived. It had as many as 1,000 there at times. Said one woman: "It was the place to be. The thing that stood out most about the building was the floor. It was built with one-inch strips, and it was so smooth and just huge. You could dance all night on that polished floor and never run into anyone… it was so huge." She marveled at the beauty of the building. "It was unequaled up here. There wasn't anything like it. Everything wasn't set up in a straight line. It had a unique design and was comfortable. It had atmosphere," she added. Jack Kotter, a member of Gary Greenfelder's One Beat Back band, sent the information about the ballroom.

Freddie Martin, a likeable Cleveland saxophone demonstrator music stores as looking for a group to substitute for his band on an engagement he heard the newly formed Martin band and recommended Freddie for the gig. The night went very well, dancers and listeners said, and Freddie, who had taken a classical selection from Tchaikovsky's B-flat piano concert, introduced a song with lyrics that became a top hit for Martin band. The new number? Freddie's beautiful Tonight We Love.

Local newspapers can be a treasuretrove of memories. A reader in eastern Pennsylvania, for example, asked about whether Duke Ellington ever played at the Sunset Ballroom, East Carrollton, PA. *AskMetaFilter* (www.ask. metafilter.com) gave a response sometime later. Did Duke play the Sunset?

It seems he did. At a dance date, June 1, 1957, and it was recorded. The response noted that Duke had his veterans with him and a recording was made that night. The veterans? Ray Nance and Clark Terry on trumpets; Quentin Jackson on trombone, Jimmy Hamilton, Johnny Hodges, Russell Procope, Paul Gonsalves and Harry Carney on saxophones and Sam Woodyard on drums.

Coconut Grove   Photo courtesy of Wikipedia.org

The response even gave the numbers played during the evening. Duke's itinerary? *Take the A Train, Such Sweet Thunder, Frustration, Cop Out, Perdido, Mood Indigo, Bassment, Sophisticated Lady, Stardust, Jeep's Blues, All of Me, I Got It Bad and that Ain't Good, On the Sunny Side of the Street.* It proves that nothing goes unnoticed and memories linger forever.

The Sunset was one of the nearly a dozen clubs, inns and hotels located nearby.

Johnny Vaselenak and his Orchestra played many times from the 1930s to the late 1990s to at the ballroom as did Johnny Vass and his orchestra.

The era that most eighty year olds miss? According to those I talk to, they remember the posh hotels such as New York's Waldorf Astoria, Lexington, Pierre, Taft, Roosevelt, the Central Park Casino, the Rainbow Room atop Radio City, Chicago's Palmer House and the Coconut Grove in Los Angeles. The pay for playing in such a style for such society audiences who could dance was "handsome," said one veteran of the day. What bands were in demand? Lombardo, Welk, Sammy Kaye, Eddy Duchin, Dick Jurgens and Freddy Martin.

1. Woody Herman Remembered, Leisure Video, 1991
2. Alan Glasscock, email Aug. 10, 2010
3. www.satinballroom.com/etiquette.htm
4. Notes, letter from Chuz Alfred, Feb. 12, 2010
5. Steve Cooper, email, Aug 24, 2010
6. Lupton's Graceland Ballroom: Hideout of Choice by Mary DeMott and includes information from the Rose City Area Historical Society
7. Ron Smolen, email, Aug 26, 2010

Acknowledgments

All readable and thought provoking books have a genesis that not only comes from the author's creative energy it also comes from people around him .

I've been blessed during my more than five decades of writing for the inspiration brought to me by women who have motivated me musically.

My late wife Patty was my life for 53 and a half years of a beautiful, loving and caring marriage and she made me promise to finish this manuscript which germinated some five years before she passed away in November, 2009, of Ovarian cancer. She fine-tuned and polished my life as a writer. She critiqued thoughts and word selections and volumes of my work   While she was never fond of my music and only heard me play once or twice during my years in the big bands, she read all my manuscripts and drafts of earlier band books. Patty was my "editor" during our years together. She answered my protests about her proposed changes with the retort: "You ASKED me to do this and you can do it yourself anytime you want!" It silenced me every time. Her innocence about "swing" music was my strength because she challenged me to provide better descriptions and precise answers to questions the reader would ask. She was a patient taskmaster and she remained so in my mind while I worked on this book. It was why I was hopelessly in love with Patty Beaty Behrens.

Given all the material that was sent to me (hundreds of photos, emails and letters) from throughout the country after the publication of Big Bands & Great Ballrooms (AuthorHouse 2006) I simply had to do this book. But writing it was a far more emotional experience than other manuscripts I've done. That's because Patty wasn't here to cajole, encourage and edit . Her satisfaction was always my satisfaction . Her standards were high like every good editor I've met and she forced me to meet them. My eyes today aren't what they were but I heard her words and voice throughout this process reminding me of what I had to do as I wrote each page . You be judge.

Thanks go to a number of people who helped me complete this book possibly without realizing their influence and impact upon me.

Faye Kline, a good friend, a big band enthusiast who with her late husband Sandy danced away the nights to bands at ballrooms in major cities offered her memories and her excitement for wonderful evenings on a dance floor.

Another good friend, a neighbor of several decades, Dee Gurdo, also encouraged me to finish this book. She loves Frank Sinatra but she also loves the sounds of big bands. When Dee and I exchanged thoughts at a neighborhood party six months after Patty's passing I was at a low point in my life. I was questioning whether this was a worthwhile task . . .whether I had the perseverance to do the months of more research and writing after editing and writing 19 full length manuscripts . She gently reminded me that Patty would have wanted me to complete this . Dee and her late husband Tony loved to dance to the big bands and her memories and enthusiasm for days past were contagious.

My kids, "foster" kids and sisters played integral parts too. Cindy and Fred Daugherty, my daughter and son in law, and my son, Mark, and his wife Nicky, contributed ideas and thoughts for "dad's music." Family support also came from my sister, Beverly Hietikko, the first "girl" singer on a high school garage band formed in a neighbor's basement, and Patty's sisters Nancy Hawkins and Judy Landis.

Two beautiful young people Patty and I met at Utica College, Kathy and Bill Randall, are the "foster children" who have helped me remain independent and continue my life.

Thanks also to a young man of many talents who has created the design and layout of my big band books, Stephen Lisi. Without him, the ideas would have been in disarray, the final product only a dream.

Along the way, of course, there were musical friends of my past in Ohio, West Virginia, Michigan, Minnesota, Pennsylvania, Iowa, Illinois, Florida, California and New York who made this third big band book a reality.

Musician friends like Chuz Alfred, Jim Booker, the late Lou DiSario, Mike Berkowitz, Ron Smolen, Steve Cooper, Alan Glasscock, California-based Gordon Goodwin and his dynamic Big Phat Band, Henry Mason of North Carolina, an energetic young bandleader named Joe Enroughty of Virginia, Gary Greenfelder of Detroit, Jack Kotter of Troy, MI., Chris Walden, another Californian; NBOEA President John Matter, Monk Rowe, Stephen Little, a disk jockey who played no instrument but loved the music, Dave Dodrill; the late Frank Galime, Al Nerino, a Penn State friend and musician; John Ghrist of the Midwest Ballroom program at WDCB radio, Chicago, the late Harold Whittemore, a newspaper editor who loved big band music and Robert Whittemore, a deejay and devotee of big band music. Nor will I forget the "band of brothers" who gathered every Friday night to play a YMCA dance in Lancaster, OH

And a special thanks to families who took the time to send me photos and memories of their loved ones. I'm grateful to Mary DiSario, widow of my longtime pen pal Lou, and Heidi Cornehis, Jill Bartlett and Richard Sievers, who helped me tell their stories of bandleader Red Sievers. Red's band was a family affair as were others like Guy Lombardo, Tommy and Jimmy Dorsey and Ray Anthony to name a few.

All of us love the sounds of big band music. All of us want the big band music to continue . . . but most of us are fearful it will not. I urge you to support your community big bands by attending performances and contributing to their causes. Make your voices heard on local radio and in other media. Community musicians, local orchestras, jazz and dance bands need your energy. . . your support. Let me know your thoughts about big band music and your memories.

There is always the chance for another big band book!

John "Jack" Behrens
Clinton, NY
www.writerjackweb.com

by John "Jack" Behrens

About the Author

Writing became my creative outlet as I stepped out of college. Degrees from Bowling Green, Penn State and post-grad work at Marshall were important but certainly professional work at Pacific Stars & Stripes, The Associated Press, Lancaster Eagle-Gazette (OH), Columbus Dispatch (OH) and later as a columnist/writer at magazines like Elks, American Printer, Financial Weekly, Nieman Reports, US Oil Weekly, Radio & TV Weekly, Mankind ,American Forests, Business Journal, Writer's Digest, Accent on Living, Physician's Financial News, American Journalism History, AOL and editing a pioneering national publication called HomeBusiness Journal, Laubach's Literary Advance , Munson-Williams-Proctor Institute (NY) Biennial Series, and Commerce Commentary gave me the life pedigree that formed and seasoned me. Today I write and edit a web site www.writerjackweb.com that attracts 25,000 hits and contribute to several national publications.   My books in the last half of the 20th century and beginning of the 21st century took more than a decade to research and write but they were worth it. I wrote Pioneering Generations: The Utica College Story, 1946-1996; Presidential Profiles for OCHS, Big Band Days: A Memoir and Source Book in 2003 and followed with the 2nd big band book in 2006 called Big Bands & Great Ballrooms: America Is Dancing. . . Again.

I authored earlier books entitled The Writing Business, Reporting, and Magazine Writing with Alex Haley

I was the founder and moderator of the UC Roundtable, a radio talk and big band show in Central New York and I started the national Student Press Archives at Utica College. I served as a Reader's Digest Foundation professor at UC teaching magazine.

Writing continues to be a way of life for me. . .   Thanks for reading.

Index

1st Herd 11

12 Cotton Club Boys 36

Abbott & Costello 84

Abe Lyman 88

Abe Lyman Orchestra 119, 121

Abraham Arden Brill 7

Ace Brigode Band 119

Ace Brogode 86

Admiral Byrd 46

A Donahue Band 122

Alan Glasscock 7, 70, 112, 128, 146

Alan Greenspan 100

Al Capone 46, 141

Al Cooper Orchestra 122

Al Croft 6

Al Donahue 81

Alex Hart 133

Al Hudson 76

Al Mastren 65

Al Nerino 91, 147

Al Nichols 59

Alvino Rey 88, 96

Alvino Rey Orchestra 118

Aly Baba 40

Ambassador 135

Ambassador Hotel 68

Ambrose and his Orchestra 125

A.M. Brown 49

Andrew Karzas 44

Andrews Sisters 119

Andy Kirk Orchestra 120, 125

Andy Williams 6

Anna Mae Winborn 76

Anna Mae Winborn and the Cotton Club
        Boys 76

Anna Mae Winburn 36

Ann Rutherford 6

Anson Weeks 88

Anthony Reichert 50

Antonini Orchestra 65

Apollo 32

Apollo Theatre 74

Aragon 45, 48, 86, 94, 95

Aragon Ballroom 34, 44, 135

Arcadia 46

Archie Bleyer Orchestra 119, 125

Art Bronson's Bostonians 33

Art Carney 96

Art Hickman 18

Art Hickman Orchestra 124

Arthur Murray 8, 39, 41

Artie Shaw 9, 18, 19, 29, 33, 35, 37, 43,

54, 65, 73, 114, 116, 135
Artie Shaw Orchestra 123, 137
Artie Shaw's Grammercy Five 37
Art Kassel 80
Art Kassell Orchestra 120
Art Mooney 43
Art Mooney Band 121
Art Mooney Orchestra 124
Astor Hotel 134
Austin Wylie 18, 33
Auturo Sandoval 10
Avalon Ballroom 40
Balboa Beach 14
band of brothers 147
Barclay Allen Orchestra 120
Barney Rapp 5
Barney Rapp Orchestra 125
B.A. Rolfe 8, 35
Ben Bernie 88, 95
Ben Birnie 133
Ben Birnie Orchestra 121
Ben Cutler 134
Beneke 75
Bennie Moten 73
Benny Carter Orchestra 122
Benny Goodman 20, 29, 30, 32, 33, 37,
    41, 43, 47, 54, 59, 63, 73, 84, 89,
    93, 100, 103, 106, 109, 112, 113,
    114, 115, 116, 117, 136
Benny Goodman Orchestra 122
Benny Goodman Quartet 37
Ben Pollack Orchestra 125
Ben Selvin 81, 88
Bernie Cummins Orchestra 120
Bert Lown Orchestra 119
Betty Evans 93
Betty Hutton 9
Beverly Hietikko 146
Big Crosby, 124
Big Phat Band 77, 139, 146
Bill Clifford Band 123
Bill Clinton 96
Bill Finegan 11

Bill Harrington 134
Billie Holiday 74, 111
Bill Karzas 45
Bill Randall 146
Billy Bishop Orchestra 118
Billy Butterfield 19
Billy Butterfield Band 126
Billy Byers 35
Billy Eckstine 6
Billy May 21, 27, 32, 35, 44, 48
Billy May Band 122
Billy Strayhorn 35
Biltmore 18
Bing Crosby 33
Bix Beiderbecke Orchestra 121
Blackhawk Restaurant 95
Blue Barron 13, 29, 31, 80, 81, 88
Blue Barron Orchestra 124
Blue Note 13
Blue Room 64
Bob Allen 81
Bob Astor Band 118
Bob Bechtel 102
Bob Brookmeyer 35
Bobby Byrne 11, 19, 29, 87
Bobby Byrne Orchestra 120, 123
Bobby Hackett 96
Bobby Hackett Orchestra 120
Bobby Sherwood Band 120
Bob Calame 77
BobCats 43
Bob Chester 52
Bob Chester Band 124
Bob Crosby 29, 43, 116
Bob Crosby Band 125
Bob Eberle 52
Bob Gioga 26
Bob Graettinger 14
Bob Hope 135
Bob Hope USO 109
Bob Montesano Sr 52
Bob Strong Band 125
Bob Wrege 6

Boyd Raeburn Band 122
Boyd Senter 135
Boyd Senter Orchestra 119
Boy Trumpet Wonder 8
Brooks Tegler 37
Bubber Miley 74
Buck Clayton 74
Buddy Boldin's Original Jazz Orchestra 17
Buddy Morrow Band 121, 123
Buddy Rich 20, 41, 43, 52, 72, 103, 107,
    108, 109, 110, 115, 139
Buddy Rich Band 61, 107
Buddy Rogers 88
Buddy Rogers Orchestra 123
Buddy Tate 74
Bugs Moran 136
Bunny Berigan 50, 73
Bunny Berigan Orchestra 121
Byrd Ballroom 45
Cab Calloway 52, 81, 111
Cab Calloway Orchestra 122, 137
Café Bohemia 131
Café Rouge 43, 44
Camel Caravan 63
Candy Toxson 61
Cannonball Adderly 131
Carl "Deacon" Moore 81
Carleton Coon 114
Carl Ravazza 81
Carl Ravazza Band 126
Carl Schreiber 46
Carmen Cavallaro 31, 81
Carmen Cavallaro Orchestra 123
Carmen Cavallero 88, 98
Carnegie Hall 115
Carole Crimmons 93
Carolyn Walters Ziebell 66
Casino Gardens 25
Castle Garden 8
Cedar Point Ballroom 48
Central Park Casino 142
Central Theater 29
Chan Chandler 76

Charles Elgar 46
Charles Elgar and his Orchestra 46
Charley Agnew Orchestra 124
Charley Barnet 32, 48
Charley Parker 132
Charley Shavers 140
Charley Spivak 11, 31, 72, 133
Charley Spivak Band 125
Charley Spivak Orchestra 61
Charlie Barnet and his Orchestra 95
Charlie Barnet Band 119
Charlie Baum 81
Charlie Spivak 13, 91
Charmot Ballroom 67
Chermont 68
Chick Webb 32, 33, 41, 50, 55, 111, 139
Chick Webb Orchestra 122
Chip Davis 35
Christopher Popa 20, 25, 90, 117, 131
Chris Walden 147
Chuck Foster 52, 80, 116
Chuck Foster Band 123
Chuck Lee 131
Chuck Robinette 141
Chummy Macgregor 65
Chuz Alfred 23, 39, 112, 131, 139, 140,
    146
Cicero Cotton Club 46
Cindy Daugherty 146
Ciro's 135
Clambake Seven 37
Claremont Hotel 96
Clark Smith 133
Clark Terry 142
Claude Hopkins 81
Claude Hopkins Band 121
Claude Thornhill 13, 15, 29, 33, 65
Claude Thornhill Band 125
Cliff Hall 99
Clyde Hurley 65
Clyde McCoy 29, 43
Clyde McCoy Orchestra 125
Coconut Grove 53, 68, 142

Coleman Hawkins Orchestra 118
Cole Porter 116
Connie Haines 52, 73
Conrad Hilton 134
Coon-Sanders Orchestra 123
Coon-Sanders Original NightHawk Orchestra
     95
Cootie Williams 74
Corky Corcoran 72
Cotillion Hall 42
Cotton Club 32, 33, 34, 40, 112, 139
Count Basie 34, 42, 43, 47, 64, 70, 73,
     74, 95, 100, 111, 114, 136
Count Basie and his Barons of Rhythm 73
Count Basie and his Orchestra 95
Count Basie Orchestra 123, 137
Crystal 51
Crystal Ballroom 42, 50, 52, 137
Dad Watson 42
Dale Brodie Band 125
Dale McMickle 65
Dan Russo 94, 114
Dave Brubeck 97
Dave Clark Five 42
Dave Dodrill 111, 147
Dave Garroway 128
Dave Matthews 72
Davey Tough 72
David Miller 30
Dean Hudson Orchestra 123
Dean Martin 6, 10, 135
Dee Gurdo 146
Del Clayton 76
Del Courtney 80
Del Courtney Orchestra 120, 125
Del Howard 18
DeMarco Dance Band 91
Desi Arnez Orchestra 119
Detroit Yacht Club 23
Dick Barne Orchestra 119
Dick Fidler Band 124
Dick Gasparre Orchestra 126
Dick Gerhart 20

Dick Haymes 19
Dickie Wells 74
Dick Johns 51
Dick Jurgen 116
Dick Jurgens 28, 29, 45, 81, 88, 95, 132,
     134, 143
Dick Jurgens Orchestra 120, 137
Dick Orange 83
Dick Sinclair 53, 68
Dick Stabile 132, 135
Dick Stabile Orchestra 118
Dick Trimble 16, 24, 90, 101
Dick Trimble Orchestra 123
Dick Westbrook 102
Dick Wickman Band 121
Dick Yeakel 8
Dizzy Gillespie 15, 132
Doc Peyton 88
Doc Severinsen 29, 104
Don Cantwell 35, 118
Don Chiesta Band 122
Don Fagerquist 108, 109
Don Glasser Orchestra 126
Don Redman 35, 47, 87
Don Redman Orchestra 119
Don Reid 89
Doobies 117
Dorothy Claire 87
Drew Savage 136
Duke Collegians 84
Duke Ellington 32, 35, 43, 52, 64, 70,
     95, 100, 105, 106, 111, 112, 142
Duke Ellington Orchestra 25, 120, 137
Dukes of Dixieland 43
Dwight Eisenhower 96
Earl "Father" Hines Orchestra 120
Earl Gardner 77
Earl Hines 95
Eddie Condon 23, 33
Eddie Derange Orchestra 120
Eddie Duchin 29, 86, 98
Eddie Duchin and his Orchestra 80
Eddie Duchin Orchestra 123

Eddie Durham 74

Eddie Howard 81, 98, 116, 134

Eddie Howard Band 119

Eddie Sauter 35

Eddy Duchin 143

Eddy Haywood Band 119

Eddy Howard 13, 31, 88, 95

Ed Gabel 26, 62

Edgar Hayes Orchestra 120

Edgar McEntree 75

Edgewater Beach Hotel 94, 114

Edgewater Park 41

Ed Morgan 22

Edmund George "Red" Sievers 59

Edward DeVincenzo 41

Edward G. Robinson 114

Edward Kennedy "Duke" Ellington 7, 74

Elgart Sound 11

Eliot Lawrence 88

Elisha Moseley 41

Ella Fitzgerald 32, 55, 84, 111, 118

Ella Fitzgerald and her Famous Orchestra 32

Elliot Lawrence Band 121

Emery Deutsch 81, 86

Emil Coleman 80, 88

Emil Flindt Orchestra 123

Enoch Light 81

Enoch Light Orchestra 126

Eric Madriguera 81

Ernie Hecksher 81, 88

Ernie Hoist Orchestra 120

Errol Garner 19

Errol Garner Trio 122

Erskine Hawkins Orchestra 124

Ethan Hay 40

Evelyn Kaye Klein 35

Ev Hoagland 80

Eydie Gorme 8

Famous Door 114

Fats Waller 111

Fats Waller Orchestra 118

Faye Kline 146

Ferde Grofe Orchestra 123

Fletcher Henderson 32, 33, 47, 50, 84, 111, 113, 117, 136

Fletcher Henderson Band 119

Florenz Ziegfeld 18

Folies Bergere 64

Four Brothers 73

Four Freshmen 6

Francis Craig Orchestra 124

Frank Bettencourt Band 120

Frank Dailey 44, 87, 92, 114

Frank D'Annolfo 65

Frank DeVol Orchestra 120

Frank Galime 24, 147

Frankie Carle 25, 81, 88, 95, 96

Frankie Carle Band 124

Frankie Catoe 94

Frankie D'Annolfo 44

Frankie Laine 6

Frankie Masters 81

Frankie Masters Orchestra 125

Frank Sinatra 6, 10, 33, 43, 52, 73, 83, 146

Fred Daugherty 146

Freddie Frink 99

Freddie Green 74

Freddie Martin 88, 142

Freddie Martin Orchestra 125

Freddie Slack 11, 81

Freddie Slack Band 125

Freddy Hinkel Orchestra 119

Freddy Martin 53, 68, 86, 116, 143

Fred Miller 91

Fred Waring 88, 115

Fred Waring Orchestra 125

Fred Workman 51

Frolics Ballroom 8

Gary Greenfelder 10, 23, 147

Gary Greenfelder's One Beat Back 142

Gary Strauss 41

Gene Krupa 13, 15, 19, 43, 52, 63, 71, 86, 107, 108, 109, 110

Gene Krupa Band 6, 107

Gene Krupa Orchestra 101, 118, 137
Geneva-on-the-Lake 48
George Ames Orchestra 119
George Eastman 17
George Gershwin 108
George Hall Band 122
George Simon 73, 113
George T. Simon 79
George W. Bush 96
Georgia Carroll 81
Georgie Auld 81
Georgie Auld Band 121
Geraldine Wyckoff 38
Gil Evans 35
Gill Emerson Orchestra 126
Ginny Simms 81, 84
Ginny Sims 133
Glendora 68
Glendora Ballrooms 135
Glen Gray 31, 62
Glen Gray Orchestra 125, 126
Glen Island Casino 13, 25, 44, 75, 87, 114
Glenn Miller 7, 9, 10, 15, 20, 21, 22, 27, 32, 37, 43, 45, 50, 64, 65, 71, 72, 76, 84, 85, 87, 89, 93, 101, 110, 111, 114, 128, 132, 133, 134, 135
Glenn Miller Alumni Orchestra 6
Glenn Miller Orchestra 53, 64, 71, 101, 122, 137
Gloria Parker 36
Gordon Goodwin 35, 77, 139, 146
Gordon Jenkins 35
Gordon MacRae 96
Grace Berrie 135
Graceland Ballroom 141
Grammercy Five 37
Grand Theatre 18
Grass Roots 41
Grateful Dead 42
Gray Gordon 80, 88
Gray Gordon Orchestra 123
Graystone 41

Graystone Manor 25
Grey Gordon 80
Grey Gordon and his Tick Tock Rhythm 80
Griff Williams 95
Gunther Schuller 75
Gus Arnheim 50
Gus Arnheim Orchestra 124
Guy and his Royal Canadians 82
Guy Lombardo 12, 21, 41, 43, 59, 78, 82, 86, 88, 89, 98, 103, 131, 147
Guy Lombardo Orchestra 118, 137
Hal Kemp 86
Hal Kemp Orchestra 121
Hal McIntyre 75
Hal McIntyre Band 123
Hal McIntyre Orchestra 137
Hal Pruden Band 118
Hamid Ballroom 90
Hamid Ballrooms 89
Hank Biagini 62
Happy Felton Band 121
Harmonicats 6
Harold Whittemore 86, 147
Harriet Nelson 81
Harry Babbit 81, 133
Harry Candulla Orchestra 123
Harry Carney 142
Harry Edison 74
Harry James 13, 30, 32, 41, 43, 53, 54, 60, 63, 65, 71, 72, 106, 117, 136
Harry James Orchestra 93, 119, 137
Heidi Cornehis 147
Heigh-Ho Club 94
Helen Johns 51
Henry Busse 31, 88
Henry Halstead Orchestra 119
Henry "Hot Lips" Busse Orchestra 121
Henry Jerome 100, 116
Henry Jerome Orchestra 123
Henry King 81, 86
Henry King Orchestra 122
Henry Mancini 35
Henry Mancini Orchestra 123

Henry Mason 36, 104
Hershey Park Ballroom 8
High Society Big Band 100
Hollywood Palladium 52, 68, 72
Hooked on Swing 11
Horace Heidt 25, 88, 95
Horace Heidt Orchestra 121
Horace Henderson Band 119
Hotel Claremont 28
  Guard Room 28
Hotel Pennsylvania 43
Hour of Charm Orchestra 35
Howard Schneider 16
Hugh James 114
Ike & Tina Turner 42
Ike Turner 42
I'm Looking Over a Four-Leaf Clover 43
I'm Not Forgetting, Don Bestor Orchestra
  125
Imperial Theater 116
Ina Ray Hutton 35
Ina Ray Hutton Orchestra, 120
Indiana Ballroom 48
Ink Spots 50
Inwood Pavilion 138
Irving Aaronson Orchestra 119
Irving Mills 35
Irv Shribman 75
Isham Jones 19
Isham Jones Orchestra 126
Ish Kabibble 82
Jack Denny Orchestra 126
Jack Fina 81
Jack Fina Band 124
Jackie Cooper 52
Jackie Mills 72
Jack Jenny 18, 19
Jack Jenny Orchestra 119
Jack Kotter 142, 147
Jack Palmer 73
Jack Palmer Band 121
Jack Russell 77
Jack Russell and his Sweet Rhythmic Orches-

tra 77
Jack Sandmeier 31
Jack Sperling 65, 109, 139
Jack Teagarden 19, 28
Jack Teagarden Orchestra 121
James Brown 42
James Petrillo 21
James Ronan 137
Jan Campbell 88
Jan Garber 12, 16, 31, 80, 86, 88, 95,
  116, 134
Jan Garber Orchestra 123, 137
Jan Savitt Orchestra 124
Jay McShann 81
Jay North 110
Jazz Vespers 115
Jefferson Beach's Pavilion 41
Jerry Gray 31, 95
Jerry Gray Band 120
Jerry Jerome Band 118
Jerry Lewis 135
Jerry Mosher 76
Jerry Wald Band 119
Jessica Luck 11
Jess Stacy 115
Jess Stacy Orchestra 120
Jill Bartlett 59, 147
Jim Booker 62, 146
Jim Ellis 43
Jimmie R. Gibbons 117
Jimmy Carter 59, 96, 104
Jimmy Dorsey 9, 15, 37, 43, 51, 59, 63,
  65, 71, 100, 104, 136, 147
Jimmy Dorsey Orchestra 119, 137
Jimmy Grier Orchestra 122, 123
Jimmy Hamilton 142
Jimmy Joy Orchestra 125
Jimmy Lunceford 32, 33, 64
Jimmy Lunceford Orchestra 120, 122
Jimmy Palmer 43, 133, 134
Jimmy Palmer Band 121
Jimmy Rushing 74
Jimmy "Scat" Davis Orchestra 121

Joan Mowery 68
Joe Bushkin 29
Joe Bushkin Band 123
Joe Delaney 64
Joe Enroughty 77, 83, 131
Joe Haymes Orchestra 123
Joe Reichman 81
Joe Sanders Orchestra 114
Joe Venuti 81
Joe Venuti Orchestra 122
John Garcia Gensel 115
John Ghrist 127, 147
John Hammond 73
John Jackaman 105
John Matter 46, 55, 129, 147
Johnny Bothwell 81
Johnny Bothwell Band 124
Johnny Catron 53, 68
Johnny Green 81
Johnny Green Orchestra 119
Johnny Hamp Orchestra 123
Johnny Hodges 74, 142
Johnny Long 84, 86, 88
Johnny Long Orchestra 125
Johnny Mercer 65
Johnny Messner Orchestra 119
Johnny Richards 35
Johnny Vaselenak 142
Johnny Vass 142
John Paul Jones Orchestra 76
John Petters 108
Jo Jones 74
Judy Garland 93, 111
Judy Landis 146
Julia Galas 45
June Christie 51
June Christy 14
Kansas City Night Hawks 114
Karim Aga Khan 97
Kate Smith 111
Kathy Randall 146
Kay Kyser 30, 45, 48, 81, 88, 95, 133
Kay Kyser Orchestra 125

Kay Thompson 19
Keely Smith 66
Keith Beecher Band 123
Kel Murray 113
Kenny Carpenter 24, 109
Kenny Mann 98
Kenny Trimble 80
Kes Hite Orchestra 122
Kevin Moran 94
Kings of Tempo 48
Kyser Orchestra 81
Lake Breeze Hotel 50
Lake Park Pavilion 51
Lakeside Ballroom 48
Larry Clinton 88
Larry Clinton Orchestra 120
Larry Elgart 10
Larry Elliott 76
Larry Faith 134
Larry Green Band 123
Las Vegas Desert Inn 25
Lawrence Welk 13, 31, 37, 38, 53, 67, 68, 80, 86, 88, 94, 134, 143
Lawrence Welk Orchestra 118
Lee Barron 60
Lee Castle 43, 88
Lee Knowles 65
Lee Williams 76
Leighton Noble 81
Lena Horne 111
Lennie Herman Band 123
Lenny Hayton Orchestra 125
Leo McElroy 53, 68
Leonard Feather 12
Leonard Garment 100
Leon Belasco Orchestra 126
Leon Merion's Big Band 140
Leo Reichert 50
Leo Walker 9, 117
Les Brown 21, 41, 51, 63, 139
Les Brown and his Band of Renown 135
Les Brown Band of Renown 109
Les Brown Orchestra 120

Les Brown's Band of Renown 137
Les Elgart 10
Les Elgart Band 121
Les Elgart Orchestra 137
Lester Lanin 41, 80, 88, 96, 97, 98, 103, 104, 134
Lester Lanin Orchestra 137
Lester Young 73, 74
Lew Quadling 94
Lexington 142
Liberty Records 63
Lindia Sievers 59
Lionel Hampton 52, 64, 109, 111
Lionel Hampton Band 120
Liquid Pleasure 98
Little John Beecher 77
Liz Varney 45
Lombardo 31
Lombardo Orchestra 90
Lou Breeze Orchestra 118
Lou Bring Band 122
Lou Cornehis 147
Lou DiSario 5, 22, 28, 65, 89, 106, 146
Louie Armstrong 43, 70, 104
Louie Armstrong Orchestra 124
Louie Bellson 109, 139
Louie Jordan and his Tympany Five 119
Louie Prima Band 118
Louie Prima Orchestra 66, 124
Louis Armstrong 52, 73, 115
Louis Brecker 47
Louis Prima 13
Louis Prima Orchestra 122
Lou King 5
Lou Marini 35
Lucky Millender 71
Lucky Millender Band 126
Lush Life Music 71
Lyndon Elks Club 6
Madura's Danceland 127
Majestic Theater Orchestra 8
Make Believe Ballroom 72
Mal Hallett 19, 33

Mal Hallett Orchestra 118
Manhattans 41
Manhattan Transfer 71
Mannheim Steamrollers 35
Manny Green 94
Marc Myers 37
Maria Schneider 35
Marigold Ballroom 67
Marion Hutton 9
Marion McKay 48
Marion McKay's Kings of Tempo 48
Martiere 141
Martin Block 72
Marvelettes 41
Marvin Frederic Orchestra 120
Marvin Gaye 42
Mary DiSario 147
Mary Louise DeMott 135
Marylou Whitney 99
Matter Ballroom 46
Maurice Ludwig 49, 52
Maynard Ferguson 10
Maynard Ferguson Band 121
Meadowbrook 8, 44, 72, 87, 92, 114
Melodears 35
Melody Mill Ballroom 134
Mel Torme 61, 64
Memo Bernabei Band 123
Meyer Davis 80, 81, 88, 134
Michael Berkowitz 6, 101
Mickey Bride 76
Mickey Scrima 72
Mike Berkowitz 107, 109, 110, 118, 146
Mike Douglas 82
Mildred Bailey 9, 73
Miller 86
Million Dollar Pier 5, 106
Milt Bernhart 25
Milt Herth Band 119
Mitchell Ayers 81
Mitchell Ayers Orchestra 126
Modernaires 136
Moe Purtill 110

Mohawk Armory 75

Molly Kathryn Sievers 67

Monk Rowe 147

Mon Rowe Band 125

Montrose Ringler 42

Mo Purtell 44

Morton Downey 9

Moseley's On The Charles 41

Muehbach Hotel 114

Mugsy Spanier Band 124

Musical Knights 91

Nancy Hawkins 146

Nat Brandwynne 81

Nat Brandwynne Orchestra 121

Nat Hentoff 12

Nat Towles 76

NC Revelers 36

Neal Hefti 35, 72

Neal Hefti Band 119

Neal Smith 99

Nelson Riddle 11, 35

Nelson Riddle Band 110

Nelson Riddle Orchestra 137

New McKinney's Cotton Pickers 140

Oak Ballroom 49

Old Roosevelt Hotel 40

Oliver Nelson 35

One Beat Back 10

Orange Blossoms 62

Oriole Orchestra 114

Orrin Tucker 29, 81, 88

Orrin Tucker Orchestra 120

Orville Knapp 80

Ozzie & Harriet Nelson Orchestra 118

Ozzie Nelson 32, 81, 88

Paddy Harmon 46

Palladium 34, 135

Palmer House 73, 95, 142

Palomar Ballroom 47, 112, 136

Palomar Theater 32

Pancho 81

Paradise Restaurant 44

Paramount Theater 61

Pat Cooper 41

Patty Beaty Behrens 145

Paul Chambers 131

Paul Gonsalves 142

Paul Kumler 24

Paul Neighbors Band, 122

Paul Pendarvis Orchestra 122

Paul "Pops" Whiteman 9, 18

Paul Revere & The Raiders 42

Paul Tanner 64

Paul Weston 32

Paul Whiteman 31, 37, 47, 51, 88, 93,
     98, 115, 116, 136

Paul Whiteman Orchestra 124

Pekin Theater 7, 17

Persian Room 134

Pete Fountain 38

Peter Daley Band 121

Peter Levinson 48

Pete Rugolo 14, 35

Phil Harris Orchestra 124

Phil Holdman 46

Philly Joe 131

Phil Spitalny 35

Phil Spitalny and his All-Girl Orchestra 123

Pier Ballroom 12, 22, 51, 52, 108

Pier Dance Hall 48

Pierre 142

President Obama 98

Prez Prado Band 119

Prince Charles 96

Queen Elizabeth II 96

Quentin Jackson 142

Radio City 142

Rainbow Room 8, 142

Ralph Burns 35

Ralph Flanagan 11, 31, 85

Ralph Flanagan Band 121

Ralph Hawkins 72

Ralph Martiere 64, 139

Ralph Martiere Band 112

Ralph Martiere Orchestra 119, 131

Randy Brooks Band 121

Ray Anthony 29, 44, 49, 59, 65, 66, 85, 147
Ray Anthony Band 65, 126
Ray Antonini 65
Ray Block Orchestra 123
Ray Charles 42
Ray Conniff 35
Ray Herbeck Orchestra 124
Ray McKinley Band 121
Raymond Scott Orchestra 124
Ray Nance 142
Ray Noble Orchestra 125
Ray Pearl Orchestra 118
Ray Reach 35
Ray Sims 73
Red Garland 131
Red Nichols 108, 116
Red Nichols and the Five Pennies 116
Red Nichols Orchestra 126
Red Norvo 11, 73
Red Norvo Band 122
Red Perkins & his Dixie Ramblers 76
Red Rodney 65
Red Sievers 67, 147
Rev. Dale Lind 115
Richard Fisher 65
Richard Himber Band 121
Richard Sievers 67, 147
Rippling Rhythm Orchestra 27
Rita Rose 36
Ritz Carlton Hotel 114
Robert Davies 105
Robert Whittemore 147
Roger Thorpe 89
Roger Wolfe Kahn Orchestra 121
Rollie Bundock 21, 44, 65
Ronald Reagan 16
Ron Armstrong 72
Ron Smolen 138, 146
Roosevelt 142
Roosevelt Grill 82
Roosevelt Hotel 95
Roosevelt Room 31

Roseland 40
Roseland Ballroom 47, 74
Rosemary Clooney 5
Rose Room 114
Royal Canadian 83
Royal Canadians 43
Roy Eldridge Band 122
Rudy Vallee 29, 81, 94, 132
Rudy Vallee Orchestra 122
Russ Carlyle 31
Russ Carlyle Band, 125
Russ Columbo Orchestra 124
Russell Procope 142
Russell's Danceland 13, 32, 52, 75
Russ Morgan 53, 86, 88
Russ Morgan Orchestra 120, 137
Sam Donahue 24, 81
Sam Donahue Orchestra 121
Sammy Kaye 12, 31, 51, 52, 81, 86, 88, 103, 116, 133, 143
Sammy Kaye Orchestra 89, 122, 137
Sammy Nestico 35
Sammy Spears 73
Samuel Zarnocray Jr 89
Sam Woodyard 142
Sandra Kay Sievers 67
Sauter-Finegan Orchestra 120
Savoy 32, 42
Savoy Ballroom 41, 139
Savoy Sultans 33
Scott Joplin 17
Seger Ellis 81
Sentimental Journey Orchestra 31, 36, 104
Serl Frank Hutton 19
Shannon Donnelly 99
Shelly Mann 106
Shep Fields 13, 27, 80, 86, 88, 93, 95, 140
Shep Fields and his Rippling Rhythm 80
Shep Fields Orchestra 124
Sherman Armory 5
Si Zentner 63
Si Zentner Band 125

Skinnay Ennis 81

Skinnay Ennis Orchestra 121

Skitch Henderson 81

Skitch Henderson Band 118

Slapsie Maxie's Nightclub 135

Smith Ballew Orchestra 125

Sonny Burke Orchestra 119

Sonny Dunham Band 122

Sonny Greer 106

Sophisticated Swing 11

Spike Jones 81

Spike Jones Band 119

Stan Billows 50

Stan Kenton 12, 19, 26, 30, 31, 33, 51, 62, 63, 80, 100, 103, 106, 139

Stan Kenton Band 62, 118

Stanley Theater 75, 93

Stardust 8

Steel Pier 8, 22, 42, 43, 89

Stephen Lisi 146

Stephen Little 105, 147

Steve Cooper 83, 116, 133, 146

Steve Knopper 117

Steve Sample Sr 35

Strand Theater 87

Sully Mason 82

Sunset 142

Sunset Ballroom 142

Sweet Rhythmic Orchestra 77

Tad Smith 74

Taft 142

Taft Hotel 36

Tanner 65

Ted Black Orchestra 124

Teddy Hill Orchestra 119

Teddy Phillips Band 122, 125

Teddy Powell Orchestra 118

Teddy Wilson 81

Ted Fio Rito 88, 114

Ted FioRito 94

Ted Fio Rito Orchestra 124

Ted G. Buckner Band 118

Ted Heath Band 122

Ted Kirby 105

Ted Lewis 37, 81, 88, 132

Ted Lewis Orchestra 126

Ted Straeter 81, 88

Ted Turner 104, 128

Ted Weems 81, 95, 132

Ted Weems Orchestra 123

Tex Beneke 7, 8, 29, 44, 53, 64, 136

Tex Beneke Band 122

Thad Jones 35

The Casa Loma Band 62

The Casa Loma Orchestra 62

The Cliff Dwellers 118

The Dorsey Brothers Band 125

The Honeydreamers 81

The Johnny Long Orchestra 84

The Oriole Orchestra 94

The Platters 41

The Revelers 104

The Royal Virginians 83

The Three Bad Habits 99

The Waldorf-Astoria Orchestra 94

The Young Sounds 6

Thurman Teague 73

Tina Turner 42

Tin Pan Alley 24

Tiny Bradshaw Orchestra 125

Tiny Hill Orchestra 118

Tiny Kahn Orchestra 122

Tom Kubis 10

Tommy Dorsey 9, 11, 15, 28, 37, 48, 51, 52, 59, 71, 73, 83, 93, 100, 104, 147

Tommy Dorsey Orchestra 121, 137

Tommy Dorsey's Clambake Seven 37

Tommy Reed Band 125

Tommy Reynolds Orchestra 124

Tommy Ryan 29

Tommy Saunders 140

Tommy Tucker 81, 88

Tommy Tucker Orchestra 121

Tony Pastor Orchestra 119, 124

Totem Pole Ballroom 54

Trianon 44, 86, 94
Tricky Sam Nanton 74
Trigger Alpert 115
Tropicana 64
Tweet Hagan Band 123
Valley Dale Ballroom 140
Van Alexander Orchestra 118
Vanity 41
Vaughn Monroe 13, 33, 81, 88
Vaughn Monroe Band 124
Verne Byers 76
Vic Damone 61
Vic Dickenson 74
Vic Schoen 35
Vic Schroeder 67
Vincent Lopez 9, 36, 81, 88, 103
Vincent Lopez Orchestra 123
Vito Musso 19
Waldorf Astoria 142
Waldorf-Astoria Hotel 114
Waldorf Astoria Orchestra 114
Walled Lake Casino 41
Walter Barnes and his Royal Creolians 46
Walter Page 70, 74
Walter Page's Blue Devils 70
Warren Covington 24, 96
Wayne Chapman 76
Wayne King 81, 88, 98
Wayne King Orchestra 98, 125
WDCB radio 147
Wilber Sweatman 7, 17, 18
Wild Bill Davidson 140
Willard Alexander 73
Will Bradley Band 125
Will Bradley Orchestra 120
Will Hollander Orchestra 121
Will Hudson Orchestra 120
William Karzas 44
Willie Bryant Band 121
Willie Farmer Band 120
Willie Schwartz 8, 44, 110, 115
Will Osborne 81, 94
Will Osborne Orchestra 125

Woodchoppers 37
Woodside Hotel 74
Woody Herman 11, 13, 19, 35, 37, 63,
    64, 72, 95, 103, 107, 115, 128
Woody Herman Orchestra 118, 137
Woody Herman's Woodchoppers 37, 107
Xavier Cugat 9, 113
Xavier Cugat Orchestra 122, 137
Yahnundasis Country Club 32
Ziegfeld Roof 18
Ziggy Elman 72
Ziggy Elman Band 118
Zinn Arthur 81
Zinn Arthur Orchestra 120